Cheeses
of South Africa

Cheeses
of South Africa

Artisanal Producers & Their Cheeses

Kobus Mulder
with Russel Wasserfall

SUNBIRD PUBLISHERS

SUNBIRD PUBLISHERS

First published in 2013

Sunbird Publishers
The illustrated imprint of Jonathan Ball Publishers
(A division of Media24 Pty Ltd)
PO Box 6836
Roggebaai 8012
Cape Town, South Africa

www.sunbirdpublishers.co.za

Registration number: 1950/038385/07

Design & typesetting by Roxanne Spears
Editor Alfred LeMaitre
Proofreader Claudia Dos Santos
Indexer Jennifer Stern

Reproduction by Resolution Colour (Pty) Ltd, Cape Town
Printed and bound by Imago

ISBN 978-1-920289-37-9

Contents

Foreword

Cheese lovers often ask me whether I prefer industrial or artisanal cheese. But what does the term 'artisan' really mean? 'Artisan' or 'artisanal' simply means that a cheese is primarily made by hand in small quantities using traditional methods and equipment – the cheesemaker uses as little mechanisation as possible. Artisanal cheeses often have unconventional shapes due to improvised moulds, may require special maturing techniques, and spices and herbs are often added. These cheeses are mostly sold in small volumes at markets to chefs, or directly to fine food retailers in the region where they are made. Traditionally – and even today, in my opinion – the expression 'farmhouse' or 'farmstead' cheese should refer to cheeses made on a farm from unpasteurised milk produced on that farm. Pasteurisation is allowed if the local authority requires it.

Both industrial and artisanal cheeses are made according to the same seven manufacturing steps, and both have a place in the food basket. Consumers should decide for themselves if they prefer industrial cheese, which often lacks individual identity due to its uniformity and homogenised flavour, or artisanal cheeses, with their more robust and complex flavours. As artisanal cheeses are handmade, it is normal, and not a defect, for the flavour and texture of the cheese to vary slightly. This is an attribute of artisanal cheeses that I expect and respect. Adventurous cheese lovers enjoy the variety of flavours and textures that artisanal cheesemakers currently offer, and they show their appreciation by buying their products.

Artisan cheese is the fastest-growing sector in the cheese market. I have been involved in the cheese industry since the days when cows could still jump over the moon, and this has afforded me opportunities to interact with artisan cheesemakers from across the globe. I have witnessed the growth of artisan cheesemaking in the United States, Wales and Ireland, and Africa. The newest area for artisan cheesemaking is East Africa, where I have been teaching cheesemaking to industrious women and men who own not more than one cow. In Mozambique, Tanzania, Rwanda, Uganda and Malawi, artisan cheesemaking is a powerful tool to double the income of a family from one to two dollars a day. Cheesemaking considerably improves their quality of life, and the international visitors to the many five-star hotels in game parks are happy to eat local cheeses. In France, where I live for part of the year, and where I have been training cheesemakers for the last 10 years, artisan cheesemaking has contributed hugely to the history and food culture of that magnificent agricultural country. It helps, of course, that they started making artisan cheese some 850 years ago.

South Africa's first recorded good Gouda, or sweet-milk, as it was known, was handmade by Dutch farmers in the Cape around the beginning of the 19th century and was followed by the making of Cheddar by the 1820 Settlers in what is now the Eastern Cape. By the middle of the last century, with improvements in infrastructure and transportation, demand exceeded production and cheesemaking moved away from farms into large cooperative cheese factories. It was the end of that artisan age of cheesemaking, a side business on farms that had grown into an industry. This became even more so in the years following the Second World War as cheesemaking entered the industrial age. For the next 45 years, the quality of South African cheese became infinitely better, but the variety was boring. I know; I was part of it.

In the early 1990s, farmers started contacting me about cheeses they had made in their kitchens or outbuildings. It was the beginning of the second artisan age of cheesemaking in South Africa, and I happily became involved. The quality was not always the best, but these pioneers were driven by the desire to make good new cheeses. The quality improved, and today cheese lovers can choose from a wide range of superb cheeses made across South Africa. Many of our artisan cheeses still need improvement, but the majority of them are of world-class standard. I say this with confidence because, each year, when I take South African cheeses to the cheese Olympics in the UK and the cheese Oscars in the USA, they return with bronze, silver, gold and double gold medals. On two occasions South Africa has had cheeses in the world's top ten. Forget the fact that I judge at these championships; I am not allowed near them, and my judging assignments cover Continental and South American cheeses.

Another question I am frequently asked is: which is your favourite cheese? I have a soft spot for unpretentious cheeses made from clean, raw milk with well-defined flavour profiles. Anything from a three-day-old fresh stretched-curd to a five-week-old soft washed-rind or ten-month-old hard brushed-rind cheese will do it for me. I appreciate the complex flavours in these cheeses, which are brought about by the workings of the good micro-flora in clean raw milk as well as the indigenous bacteria in the cheesery.

This book pays homage to a number of artisanal stalwarts who understand the art of cheesemaking. They are a combination of scientist and artist, with the ability to work long hours, alone, while paying attention to the detail which cheesemaking requires.

Kobus Mulder
Chevalier de l'Ordre Mérite agricole de France
Prud'homme de la Guilde des Fromagers
Officier des Chevaliers du Taste-Fromage de France

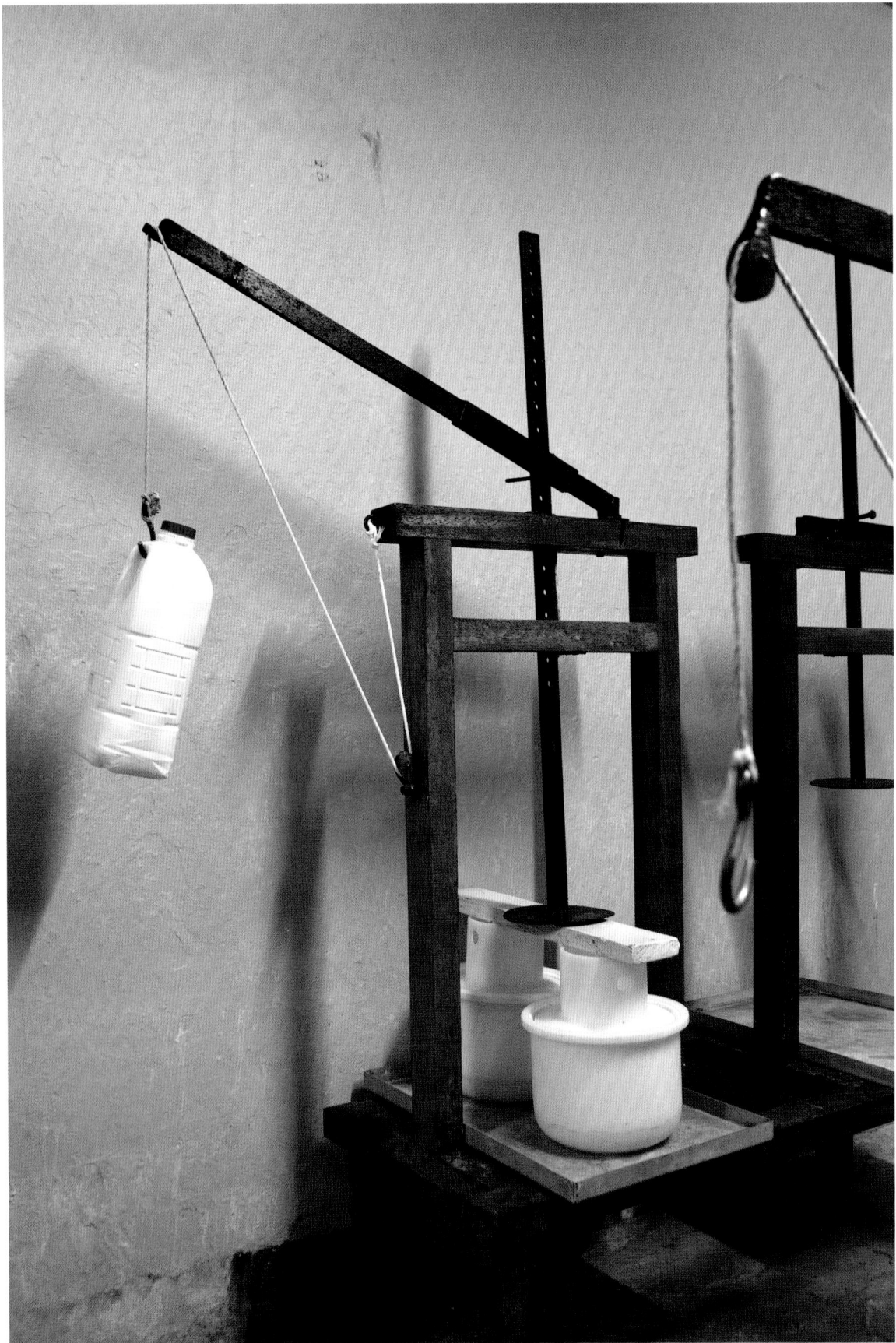

Introduction

The story of cheese goes back many thousands of years. The earliest evidence of cheesemaking comes from approximately 3 000 years ago. It is thought that the first cheeses came about more or less by accident, when milk stored in the stomach of an animal – a common method of storing foodstuffs, particularly among nomadic peoples – soured and separated into solids (curds) and liquid (whey). The development of cheese meant that highly perishable milk could be turned into a long-lasting, nourishing and tasty food.

Today, cheese is made all over the world in an extraordinary variety of shapes, styles and colours – from delicate sticks of goat's cheese coated in ash to robust and pungent blue cheeses. In fact, the enormous variety of cheese makes formal classification quite tricky (see Types of Cheeses below). The basic raw material – milk – can come from sheep, cows, goats, water buffalo and even reindeer. The flavour of the milk is influenced by the microflora present in the animal's stomach, which in turn is affected by specific local factors of soil, climate and pasturage. The concept of terroir, a French word referring to the influence of local factors on the character of wine, is certainly applicable to the production of cheese.

In recent years, South Africa has seen something of a revolution in cheesemaking. In the past, consumers had a limited range of cheeses to choose from, but the rise of artisanal cheesemaking has changed this picture. Thanks to pioneers like Wendy Harris, of Indezi River, and Chrissie Briscoe, of Chrissie's Country Cheese, there is a greater variety of cheeses available in retail stores and supermarkets, and an increased willingness on the part of cheesemakers to experiment with new tastes and styles. Consumers have also become more knowledgeable and more discerning about what they buy.

Since 1995, South Africa's per capita cheese consumption has increased from 1.0 kg to 1.9 kg, according to Agri-Expo, a dairy industry body. Moreover, consumers have embraced more unusual styles and flavours. In turn, local cheesemakers have developed new products, such as Dalewood's award-winning Huguenot, that reflect local conditions and tastes and also honour the great cheesemaking traditions of the world.

One of the key factors in this process has been the South African National Cheese Festival. The first edition of this event was held in April 2002 at Bien Donné farm outside Franschhoek. The numbers of exhibitors – and enthusiastic visitors – grew by the year, and in 2011 the festival moved to Sandringham Farm, outside Paarl.

Agri-Expo also runs the South African Dairy Championships, the country's only competitive dairy awards. The industry's symbol of excellence is the Qualité Award, which has been awarded to qualifying dairy products since 2001. Products bearing the coveted Qualité logo represent the best in local cheesemaking. The title of Dairy Product of the Year is the very pinnacle of honour for a South African dairy product, and is bestowed on the best of the Qualité Award winners.

South African cheeses have also earned acclaim at the annual World Cheese Awards, held in Birmingham under the umbrella of the BBC Good Food Show. In 2011 Kobus Mulder – 'Mr Cheese' – was himself honoured by the World Cheese Awards for his Exceptional Contribution to Cheese.

This section covers the basics of cheesemaking, the different types of milk and their characteristics and the advantages of raw versus pasteurised milk, and offers practical advice on planning a cheeseboard and how to pair cheese and wine. The bulk of the book focuses on the stories of individual cheesemakers and how they have developed their cheeses. Each chapter includes 'Cheese Notes' by Kobus Mulder, offering a personal view of the achievements of the cheesemakers and their products.

This is not a definitive encyclopaedia of artisanal cheese in South Africa. The cheese scene is constantly changing as new producers appear and interest grows in local artisanal foods. Rather, the book is a snapshot of some of the innovators and visionaries who have done so much to change the nature of cheesemaking in South Africa. Seek out their products, but look around and be willing to try the many new cheeses that you see.

Making Cheese

All cheesemaking comes down to a very simple formula, the principles of which have not changed for several thousand years. The first step in the process is known as coagulation, or curdling. This involves the separation of the milk into curds (solids, protein and fats) and whey (mainly water). Coagulation is what happens when milk curdles when left in a warm place, and occurs because bacteria turn the milk sugars (lactose) into sour milk (lactic acid). Once the desired acidity is reached, a starter culture is added to speed up the process of coagulation. The culture consists either of some slightly soured milk (usually taken from the previous day's supply) or a synthetic culture (in the case of using pasteurised milk). Too much or too little will result in an imperfect cheese, and getting the quantities right is a skill known to the cheesemaker.

Making a cheese by only using a starter culture will result in cheese that is sharp and acidic – suitable for fresh cheeses, but not matured ones. In order to make a cheese that will age well, rennet is used. Every milk-fed animal is born with a specific enzyme in the stomach which converts milk into solids and liquids, and rennet is produced from the stomach lining of animals. Rennet assists in breaking down the curd into an even consistency, which plays a role in the final outcome of the cheese. Because rennet is an animal product, some vegetarians are reluctant to eat cheese. A non-animal rennet is now produced, known as a microbial/vegetarian rennet. Certain plants, such as thistles and figs, have also been used to initiate coagulation.

The degree of coagulation determines the final moisture content of the cheese, and also plays a role in the speed of the fermentation process. At this point it is important to separate the curds from the whey. Doing this gently produces cheese that is high in moisture and soft, while cutting the curds produces harder cheeses, because this expels more whey. The finer the curd is cut, the harder the final cheese. After this process, the whey is drained from the curds.

The curds, drained of the whey, are placed in moulds, ready for pressing. Once pressed, the cheese may be rubbed with salt before it is placed in a cold room to age. It is during the aging process, or the affinage, that the flavours and character of the cheese develop.

Types of Cheese

The categorisation of cheeses is a sometimes contentious subject, and different sources of information will inevitably give different classifications. However, for the purposes of this book five basic styles of cheese are recognised, namely, fresh, soft, semi-soft, semi-hard and hard.

Fresh Cheese

Fresh cheese is noticeably white and has no rind, but holds its shape well. It is ready for consumption almost immediately after production. Fresh cheese usually has a mildly sour or sharp flavour that is similar to yoghurt and a creamy consistency, and is often favoured in pairing with fresh and raw ingredients. Although fresh cheeses have not had time to develop all of the milk's potential flavour, they are anything but bland. Of all the various types of cheese, fresh cheese has the lowest fat content and the highest moisture content. The high moisture content means that they have a very short shelf life. Fresh cheeses can also be aged, which creates a distinctive wrinkled rind, coated in moulds and yeasts. Popular examples of fresh cheese include halloumi, ricotta, feta and mascarpone. An example of an aged fresh cheese is Mouse Cheese, an aged chevin made at Cloud Cottage.

Soft Cheese (includes bloomy rind and pasta filata)

Like fresh cheese, this type of cheese has a high water content and a creamy consistency. Soft cheeses are delicate and have a short shelf life, though not as short as fresh cheese. This category of cheese also includes bloomy rind and *pasta filata* cheese.

The name 'bloomy rind' comes from the white fluffy coat (caused by the mould *Penicillium candidum*) that makes such cheeses easily distinguishable. The coat protects the cheese from drying out while it ages, and also speeds up the process of ripening. This is why these cheeses are sometimes referred to as mould-ripened cheeses. Examples of bloomy rind cheese include Camembert and Brie.

When making *pasta filata* cheese, curds are spun or stretched (the Italian term *pasta filata* means 'spun paste') before the cheese is complete. Once the curds have been drained of whey the fresh cheese is allowed to rest in hot water; then the pieces are stretched and kneaded until the correct texture is achieved. The process also plays an important role in the flavour of the cheese. Mozzarella is a good example of this type of cheese.

Semi-soft Cheese

These cheeses are slightly stronger in flavour than fresh and soft cheeses, and hold their shape much better. Colby is an example of a semi-soft cheese.

Semi-hard Cheese

Moisture is squeezed out of this type of cheese before it is shaped, and the resulting flavour is more robust. Examples of this cheese include Cheddar and Gouda.

Hard Cheese

This type of cheese has usually been aged over a considerable length of time, and has a firm, also crumbly, texture and strong flavours. Examples include Parmesan and Gruyère.

Types of Milk

Despite the differences between cheeses, they each rely on the same basic ingredient – milk. Milk contains all the vital ingredients necessary for nourishment: vital minerals, sugars, fats, vitamins, proteins, carbohydrates and nutrients. This makes it an important and substantial foodstuff in its own right – much more than just something to drink.

Different types of animal yield different types of milk, each with their own characteristics. Between breeds, too, the milk differs – for example, between Friesian and Guernsey cows. The fat content in milk depends on the breed, as well as the farming methods, the animal's own lactation phase and the milking.

Even within the same breeds, milk takes on different characteristics depending on the area. The terroir – the interaction between the grazing, the animal and the climate – plays a significant role in the final milk product. For example, in spring the pastures are typically more moist, green and sweet; this adds to the richness and flavours of the milk, which will influence the final product. Different animals also have their own grazing habits, which in turn plays a role in the final flavours. Cows, for example, feed mostly on pastures, while goats are browsers, and will eat almost anything.

An artisanal cheesemaker is the first to say that no two batches of cheese are identical. This would be impossible, as there is no way of controlling each element that plays a role in milk production. Because of this, the cheeses vary from day to day, as wine vintages do from year to year.

The production of milk does not occur all year round, but after the animal has given birth, which (unlike humans) only happens during a specific time, once a year. It is possible to control and manipulate the animals into breeding out of season, but this is not practised regularly. Cows have a relatively long lactation period; sheep and goats, on the other hand, produce milk for a much shorter period of time.

Different species of milk-producing animals produce varying types of milk, which yield different quantities of cheese. This has to do with the amount of butterfat, which is simply the fatty portion of the milk. Cow's milk has a lower proportion of butterfat to sheep's milk, and while it takes on average 10 litres of cow's milk to produce one kilogram of cheese, it takes only 5 litres of sheep's milk for the same quantity of cheese.

Guernsey Milk

Cow's milk varies from breed to breed, but the difference between Guernsey milk and milk from other breeds is considerable. Also known as A2 milk, it has several unique properties, and there has been an increasing interest in it over recent years. Interestingly, people who are lactose intolerant can consume milk with the A2 protein without side effects. Although the reports vary, only positive results have shown from a diet of A2 milk, and there is also ongoing research into whether the A1 protein may play a negative role in daily health.

A1 and A2 casein proteins are different categories of proteins, with different chemical structures. A1 B-casein protein is the most common protein found in cow's milk, while about 95% of the protein in Guernsey milk is carried in the A2 form. It is not just Guernsey milk that contains A2 protein; it is also present in goat's, buffalo and sheep's milk.

Aside from its popular flavour, another very obvious difference is that Guernsey milk has a creamy golden colour, which is created by the high level of beta carotene (a major source of vitamin A). The milk has a high butterfat and protein content, but, because it is so balanced in nutrients, it is regarded as a healthier option. Guernsey milk contains about three times the amount of omega-3 oils as milk from other breeds, and has higher levels of vitamins and calcium.

Buffalo & Their Milk

There are two types of water buffalo: the swamp buffalo (found by the million in India, but not ideally suited to milking), and the bigger riverine water buffalo, the type that is farmed in the Campania region of Italy. Buffalo are very intelligent and curious creatures. They are not malicious, although they can be protective, which can lead to aggression. Water buffalo are unrelated to the Cape buffalo, and, because they have been domesticated for centuries, they are a lot gentler than their distant African relatives. 'More than anything else', says Wayne Rademeyer of Buffalo Ridge, 'they just like to eat all day. They're like motors.' Buffalo herds are very hierarchical. 'The dominant cow is the local minister and the bull is like the foreign minister', Wayne jokes as he explains the nature of the herd. Between them, the buffalo sort out where they fit in the herd.

Buffalo is a sustainable farm animal, as the average cow has between 15 and 18 lactations in her lifetime, which means she can be worked with for about 20 years – the normal life span of the animal. The average milk yield of a buffalo is about 10 litres per day.

Buffalo milk is highly nutritious, for several reasons. It is high in protein and calcium, with over 40% more of each than cow's and goat's milk. It is also significantly lower in cholesterol than cow's, goat's or sheep's milk. Lactose-intolerant people can consume buffalo milk, it contains antioxidants and the fat it contains is beneficial. In fact, there is a 25% lower fat content in buffalo milk, which is even lower than regular 'low fat' cheese. Because there is such a high ratio of milk solids in buffalo milk, there is a much

lower milk-to-cheese ratio when using buffalo milk. To make cheese, less than half the amount of buffalo milk is needed than for cheese made with cow's milk.

The milk itself tastes very similar to cow's milk, with the difference being that it is sweeter and richer. Buffalo milk has a surprisingly long shelf life, because of a natural preservative that occurs in a much higher ratio than in cow's milk.

Sheep's Milk

Sheep have been milked for thousands of years, and dairy products were made from this type of milk long before cows were milked. Sheep's milk has a multitude of health benefits because of its composition of nutrients, most found in higher quantities than in cow's or goat's milk. It is the ideal milk for cheesemaking because, although sheep produce a smaller volume of milk than cows, it is richer in fat, minerals, vitamins and solids.

Sheep's milk is easier to digest because it contains a higher proportion of what are known as short- and medium-chain fatty acids. These are known to have little effect on cholesterol levels, unlike milk from a cow. Sheep's milk does contain lactose and protein, but most people who are allergic to cow's milk products encounter no problems with sheep's milk. This is because the lactose in sheep's milk is made up differently, and is full of enzymes that allow calcium to metabolise in our bodies.

Raw (unpasteurised) Milk vs Pasteurised Milk

It is widely believed that raw milk, rather than that which has been pasteurised, makes a more flavoursome cheese, This is due to the fact that all of the naturally occurring bacteria are lost when the milk is heated during the pasteurisation process. Heating milk kills any existing pathogens and reduces the amount of germs, but it also destroys nearly all of the microbial flora, which play an enormous role in determining the characteristic flavour of the final cheese product. Laboratory-produced cultures cannot emulate nature and the complexity of natural bacteria, so cheese made from pasteurised milk is significantly different to cheese made from raw milk.

As much as it is lauded, there are also negative connotations to raw milk and much publicity about health issues regarding unpasteurised milk. In reality, raw milk has never been proved to be harmful; if a cheese causes health problems it is because of bad hygiene practice, not the milk itself. There is evidence to show that untreated milk has a higher nutritional value than pasteurised milk. Good and bad bacteria exist in all natural products, but if the preparation of the cheese and the dairy hygiene is good, the bad bacteria will be eliminated by the good during the ripening process.

When milk is pasteurised, the natural bacteria that are lost must be replaced in order to make cheese from the milk. This is done by adding a culture (grown in laboratories) to the milk. These cultures and the numerous enzymes in the milk work on the lactose, protein and fat in the cheesemaking process.

Despite all of the talk to the contrary, there are still some exceptional cheeses that are made with pasteurised milk; cheese produced on a large scale needs to be pasteurised, so that it can be standardised in order to ensure consistent flavour, texture and appearance. When large factories produce cheese, they buy milk from a variety of suppliers, and pasteurisation ensures that no unwanted germs are included. Regulations governing cheese retailing are also difficult to negotiate if the milk is untreated.

There are several processes for pasteurising milk, but all involve the basic principle of heating the milk. These range from heating it over an extended period of half an hour at 62 °C (extended heating) to heating it for several seconds at 85 °C (high temperature heating).

Rennet

Rennet is a crucial ingredient in making cheese, but the debate over the use of animal rennet or vegetarian (microbial rennet substitute) rennet is one that has sparked much interest recently.

Legend has it that rennet was first discovered centuries ago by travelling herdsmen who kept their milk supply in a sack made from the stomach of a lamb. At the end of a day's work, they found that their milk had separated.

Rennet is an extract that contains a number of enzymes. Enzymes are, simply put, biological catalysts that drive chemical reactions in our bodies. Traditionally, rennet is extracted from the fourth stomach of young ruminants like cows, sheep or goats. The enzymes present in the animal's stomach are what makes it able to digest its mother's milk. When we add rennet to milk, it causes the milk to coagulate; this is what forms curds and whey, which is a vital step in the cheesemaking process. Rennet, therefore, cannot be replaced.

However, we can change the way in which we source the rennet. The main enzymes in rennet can be recreated in a laboratory as microbial rennet substitute. Plants and fungi are also sources of naturally occurring enzymes that can substitute for animal rennet.

The jury is still out on whether cheeses created using animal or 'vegetarian' rennet differ, and whether or not these differences are important.

Cheddaring

Cheddar cheese is known and loved around the world, but many generic 'Cheddars' that we see on supermarket shelves do not deserve their name. Cheddar is a village in Somerset, in southwest England, and it is in this area that the cheese was first created.

Making Cheddar begins in the same way as any cheesemaking: by adding culture and rennet to milk and allowing it to set, and then draining off the whey. Usually, the curds would be pressed at this point, but when making Cheddar the process changes. Water is added to the curds, which are heated and stirred continuously. Once the water has been drained, the curds are pushed to release as much liquid as possible and knit together. They are cut into blocks, piled on each other and regularly turned, which presses and drains them further. During this time, the acidity of the curds rises slightly, which preserves the cheese. Finally, the blocks are milled into small curds again before pressing them in moulds to further drain and then age. Without the cheddaring process, the cheese would not have its distinctive dense and crumbly texture nor its characteristic flavour.

Affinage, or Cheese Maturing

The microclimate of the cheese room, coupled with the type of milk, provides the last touch in a cheese's flavour. Yeasts and moulds in the air work on each batch of protein-rich curd, while inside each batch a multitude of bacteria convert the lactose into lactic acid. It is the responsibility of the affineur to take the cheese to its true potential. Each affineur has his/her own individual style which creates an impact of flavours and, in many cases, is immediately recogniseable by the cheese connoisseur. It is a true craft, just like winemaking, as the final outcome is evaluated by the senses.

There are countless aspects that influence the affineur's task. These range from variables in the milk, to variables in the cheesemaking process (which can be controlled), to variables in the climate, season and location of the storage room. Absolutely every aspect plays a role in the final product, and changing just one variable could result in an entirely different cheese.

Storing & Cutting Cheese

Once cheese is bought for consumption, there are several things to consider in order to maintain its quality and get the best taste out if it. These include the way in which a cheese is stored, and the manner in which it is cut.

Cheese is a living product that will continue to ripen once it has been bought, and there are several habits that one should get into when storing cheese. When cheese is stored in a fridge, it should ideally be in a container or on a tray that is covered with a clean and damp tea towel. Uncovered cheese should never be left in a fridge that contains raw foods, as it spoils easily. Cheese varieties with mould should be stored separately from other cheeses so that the mould does not spread. Cheese should be taken out of the fridge at least an hour before serving.

Before serving some cheeses, especially hard cheeses, they should be 'refreshed' by scraping the exposed side lightly with a sharp knife, and removing any dried or discoloured surfaces. Cut away any dried edges on soft cheeses.

It is important to protect the cut edge of a cheese from drying out without robbing it of air that it needs to breathe. Cut surfaces should ideally be covered with foil (for blue and white mould cheeses) or a breathable plastic wrap (for hard and semi-hard cheeses). Most hard and semi-hard cheese can also be stored in an airtight plastic container.

Cutting cheese is important not only for presentation but also so that the various aspects of the cheese can be enjoyed – flavour can differ from the inside to the outside, especially with bloomy rind cheeses. Round and rectangular soft cheeses should be cut like a cake, as should blue cheeses, while sticks and rolls can be cut into thick slices.

A cheese wire is a useful instrument for cutting through cheese smoothly and effortlessly, as is a standard wide-bladed cheese knife. Cheese knives with two-pronged tips are best suited to soft cheeses and small pieces, and most cheese knives should have a serrated edge, which ensures that the cheese comes away from the blade easily. Interestingly, it is better to use a blunter blade rather than a sharper one for cutting cheese, and warming the blade in hot water also makes for a smoother cut. Cheeses that are very hard should be broken and not cut at all, while cheese planes can be used for shaving thin strips from hard cheeses. Cheese graters are also well suited to harder cheeses; the larger the perforations, the better suited the grater is to softer cheeses. Specialist cheese equipment, such as the girolle (used for scraping the surface), is suited to particular types of cheese.

Creating a Cheeseboard

There are no strict rules for creating a cheeseboard, and personal taste plays a big role. Determining which type of cheese is preferred, and then balancing the cheeseboard around it, is a good way to start as it is important to have a selection of types of cheese. Diversity should be shown in texture – from creamy and smooth to hard-grained – and a cheeseboard should also always include a goat's, sheep's or buffalo milk cheese.

A classic cheeseboard would consist of five cheeses: a goat's cheese, a bloomy-rinded cheese, a hard cheese, a washed cheese and a blue cheese.

Cheeseboard accompaniments vary. A staple accompaniment is bread, of which there is a vast range to choose from. Nuts are also very common on a cheeseboard, as are pickles (or chutney). Serving savoury preserves on a cheeseboard is a very English habit, and as accompaniments they work very well with hard, mature cheeses. Fruit (fresh or dried) can also be on a cheeseboard, although citrus and tropical fruit should be avoided if the fruit is fresh. Raisins and dried figs are common accompaniments to cheese – in Spain, it is typical to be served cheese with a fruit paste made from figs, quinces, raisins and almonds – and mainly served with hard sheep's cheeses. Other options for accompaniments are olives, spring onions, fresh beans, celery and crisp greens (like rocket). For a sweeter option, honey drizzled over some cheeses is also a popular choice.

Cheese and wine

A general rule (to which, of course, there are exceptions) in pairing cheese and wine is to pair light, young cheeses with light, crisp wines. For example, a fresh cheese would be paired with a crisp and fruity white wine. A richer, soft cheese would be well-suited to a Chardonnay, or maybe a rosé. Harder and darker cheeses work better with richer, heavier wines. Blue cheeses, though, work best with sweet wines. Red wine can be a difficult partner to cheese, especially wine that is very perfumed, floral or high in tannins. Tannins in the wine can tend to 'steal' some of the subtle flavours in a cheese. Pinot Noir is a popular red wine to pair with cheese, because of its lower tannin levels. In many cases, if there is a wine that comes from the same region as a cheese, the two will invariably pair well.

Aidan Pomario

Hoekwil, Western Cape
Aidan Pomario

Perhaps it's his charming manner and his easy smile, but there is no doubting that by 8:30 on Saturday morning the queue to Aidan Pomario's stall at the Wild Oats Market in Sedgefield far surpasses any other. The market has become a well-known Saturday event in the Garden Route region. From 8 am, come rain or shine, a steady stream of visitors is standing in line at Aidan's stall. And, no, it is not (just) the charismatic man that draws them in. Aidan makes a variety of goat's cheese and Camembert that local cheese connoisseurs just can't get enough of.

At a small, 38-ha farm in Hoekwil, Aidan milks 47 Saanen goats and produces a variety of cheeses, both hard and soft. He bought the property in 2005, and lives there with his wife and daughter. Aidan originally studied as a pastry chef at the Cordon Bleu school in London, and worked as a chef in several well-known restaurants until suffering an injury in 1995. Finding himself with a lot of spare time on his hands, he became interested in cheesemaking. He experimented a little and decided to do a two-year apprenticeship at Bloublommetjieskloof, a bio-organic farm near Wellington.

Aidan thinks like a chef, and he deliberated systematically and scientifically about his cheesemaking and farming processes. He wanted to create something artisanal, and realised that the animals are as integral to the cheese as the processes used. He likes to work with goats, and believes that 'humans have an affinity with goats more than they do with cows or with sheep'. He uses raw milk when making cheese, and has chosen to use a microbial (vegetarian) rennet instead of the more common animal product.

THE GARDEN OF AIDAN

Goat's Milk
FETA

BE TEMPTED!

Goat's Milk
CHEVIN

Aidan Pomario Cheddar

Aidan Pomario Bûchette-style Chevin

He separates the male goats from the females, and keeps a close eye on the diet of the herd. The goats eat mainly lucerne, although they also graze on indigenous fynbos, pine and wattle. Aidan believes that this varied natural diet has an impact on the fat and protein content of the milk, and thus plays a large role in the flavours of his cheeses. He doesn't regulate the exact diet of his animals, so the flavour of his cheese varies, but this doesn't bother him: 'I don't make a consistent cheese, but I do make a consistently good cheese.'

About half of Aidan's monthly sales comes from the Wild Oats market, although he also sells to restaurants, delis and health shops. Many locals call him in advance to book his produce in case they don't get there before it all sells out. People know him and he remembers names. When he has a free moment, someone will go and chat to him and he'll tell them about his farm and what he's currently working on. Preparation for the Saturday market starts on Thursday, and although cheese is his main product Aidan also makes breads and a delectable cheesecake that sells out quickly.

Kobus's Cheese Notes

Thanks to Aidan Pomario the Hoekwil farming area above Wilderness is famous for goat's milk cheese and cheesecake. Aidan's road to his idyllic farm near Diep Rivier was not a shortcut. His route to a self-sufficient lifestyle was via electrical engineering, baking, the London Cordon Bleu school, the hospitality industry and a two-year stint at Bloublommetjieskloof, where he discovered a new love for cheesemaking.

Once Aidan had cleared enough of the alien tree species on the farm, he parked his caravan and got to work. He first obtained six goat kids, soon followed by more. By 2006, his first cheese, a feta, was ready for the Wilderness night market. Today, he makes a well-balanced range of cheeses, which stretches from a well-matured Cheddar to a fresh bûchette-style cheese covered in a variety of herbs and spices.

The matured Cheddar has a typical hard but slightly open texture, but it is worlds apart from the matured Cheddar available in normal retail outlets. The flavour reminds me of a farmyard, where animals roam freely and chickens scratch around for morsels of food – which is just the case at Diep Rivier Farm. Aidan's pecorino is a hard cheese that grates beautifully into small flakes, which brings a pasta dish or a green salad to new heights of flavour. Whenever I am lucky enough to have some in my fridge, I eat it with cheap imported Sangiovese wine, because it complements the watery Italian wine to such a degree that it tastes like a good red blend from Paarl.

Aidan's Camembert ripens at a remarkably early age, which is a sure sign that the milk from his goat herd is rich in the enzymes necessary to break down the flavour-giving protein. I eat it with only a thin 'heart' in the middle of the cheese, and prepare it in two ways: either I bake it with fresh garlic and rosemary, drizzle with good olive oil from the Klein Karoo and soak it up with two-day old toasted bread, or I melt the whole Camembert in the oven and then scoop it over penne pasta. Yes, I know, Giorgio Locatelli would have a fit, but he has not tasted Aidan's Camembert.

The fresh, round bûchette-style cheeses are plain or rolled in a variety of spices. I love to cut the little rolls into thin discs, grill them and enjoy my favourite *chevré chaud*. Because this is a cheese book, I am not going to mention Aidan's sourdough rye bread and various baked products made with stone-ground flour. What I will mention, though, is his legendary cheesecake. Yes, it is legendary. Otherwise, why would I drive 67 km to a coffee shop outside Wilderness with seven French guests to taste it? The cheesecake is not made with goat's milk but with Jersey cream, and was voted the Best Sweet Bakery product in 2010 by a national know-all food directory. I only have two questions: where were the judges before 2010, and why did they have to nail the news to the national notice board? On two subsequent occasions I have arrived at Café d'Afrique to find the cheesecake sold out.

Aidan Pomario Pecorino

Alpine Goats Cheese

Dragonfly Farm, Napier, Western Cape
Brenda Shelley & Jacqui Weilenmann

A short distance outside the town of Napier, in the farmlands of the Overberg region, lies the unmistakeable property of Brenda Shelley and Jacqui Weilenmann. They have made a home for themselves in one of the most beautiful parts of the Western Cape, and have designed a lifestyle around it that suits them perfectly.

It was while visiting a friend who was living in Napier that Brenda and Jacqui fell in love with the quaint little town and the countryside. They bought a rundown house, sold their city home, and moved to the country. They wanted to keep animals, and already had a horse, so they looked at other farm animals. They settled on goats, partly because Jacqui had a childhood dream of breeding goats and making cheese from their milk. They went to a farmer in nearby Bredasdorp and returned home with eight pregnant ewes and a buck. Those nine goats quickly became a herd of 23 goats, which required a larger plot. The idea was to establish a biodynamic farm – big enough to farm, but not too extensive.

They decided to build a Swiss-style farmhouse, a double-volume structure that houses animals on the ground and people on the upper level. 'People here thought we were crazy!' laughs Brenda. The night that the house was completed, the second birthing season began, resulting in their herd growing to 58 goats. The house has proved a huge success. Because the living area is right above the shed, Brenda and Jacqui have quick access to their herd at all times.

Alpine Peasant

Brenda and Jacqui feel that it is important for children, especially those that grow up in cities, to get a taste of country living and to learn how goats are milked and cheese is made, and that milk and cheese do not just come off the shelves in their local supermarket. Consequently, they regularly open their farm to the public. Because all of their goats are hand-raised, they don't mind being handled.

Today, Jacqui and Brenda keep a herd of 150 goats, and milk about 60 of them. The goats are pasture-fed, and feed on Port Jacksons, pine, lucerne, oats and hay. The milking goats are also fed a concentrate. Brenda and Jacqui keep their billies separate from the ewes, and run a very organised herd. Jacqui is also meticulous about her cheesemaking and is very careful not to contaminate the cheese with the male scent. Brenda explains that their cheese is 'ungoaty' because of this.

Kobus's Cheese Notes

Jacqui makes an unpretentious and original semi-soft peasant cheese, as well as a caciotta, which has a similar consistency to mozzarella. The cheese is produced plain, and also comes in 16 flavours. She uses a range of condiments like local herbs, olive oil, basil, oregano and garlic. Jacqui makes cheese immediately after the twice-daily milking, a labour-intensive practice that guarantees the freshest possible milk, as the milk has not had an opportunity to develop any lactic acid.

Fruit vinegar rather than rennet is used to coagulate the milk, which makes the cheese one of the very few lactic-curd cheeses in the country. To maximise the natural draining of the curds, Jacqui does not cut the coagulum, but, when firm enough, she scoops dollops into the cheese moulds, Camembert-style. This style of treating the curd ensures the optimum quantity of moisture in the cheese, delivering a clean but refreshing, slightly acidic taste. This type of cheese can be eaten after one week. With its unmatured, clean flavour, it goes well with a large range of fresh or light foods.

The texture is semi-soft with very few openings, which makes it a perfect table cheese. Picture yourself sitting on the veranda with a slice of Alpine Goats Cheese, a plate of freshly cut crudités and a fine Sauvignon Blanc – gastronomic bliss.

Alpine Caciotta

Beaconsfield

Hofmeyr, Free State
Bruce & Charles Lord

Driving into Beaconsfield farm feels like a trip into an Enid Blyton novel, where white fluffy sheep graze by the side of the road, horses eye passersby, and the bright green grass almost sparkles. Two border collies chase each other in the garden in front of the grand 200-year-old farmhouse and chickens cluck around the kitchen door. This is the home of the Lord family, where Charles and Bruce are producers of Beaconsfield sheep's milk cheese.

Beaconsfield Farm extends over 700 ha in an area that is well known for endurance riding. The farm is irrigated with water from the Gariep Dam, which ensures that the fields and pastures are lush throughout the year. The Lords run the farm on hydroelectric power and generate their own electricity from water in their dam. The majority of their sheep are East Friesian, which originated in the same region of Germany as Holstein cows and are well known for being very easy to milk. The Lords also keep local breeds, which are more difficult to milk but extremely hardy.

Charles Lord had the backing of his whole family when he decided to make sheep's cheese independently. One of the main reasons for going into cheese production was the farm's isolation. The logistics of transport make delivering anything fresh difficult, as the closest point of sale is 40 km away.

When the Lords first investigated cheesemaking, Charles's eldest son was working in Welkom, employed by a Greek who put the Lords in touch with a friend from Cyprus who had some knowledge of making halloumi. Charles and his wife, Karen, drove to

Welkom armed with litres of sheep's milk and a desire to learn. They made their first batch of halloumi with 'Mr Pappas' in his carport. Needless to say, the Lords have adapted their processes and refined their method, but the skills they learnt in Welkom that weekend have proved significant.

Charles keeps a close eye on the upkeep of his herd, and his ewes have been inseminated with sperm from Australia. The 160 sheep that they milk daily each average 500 ml of milk. Milking sheep is not as readily accepted in the area as milking cows or goats, and it has provoked some scepticism from other farmers. The Lords see the lighter side of it, though. 'If my grandfather or father knew that I was milking sheep, they wouldn't believe it,' laughs Karen, 'now I can't help looking at sheep's udders when I visit another farm. Milking sheep has become so normal to us.'

The dogs herd the sheep to the kraal at milking times. They know when to fetch them, and if the farming staff are late, the dogs become anxious. 'I don't understand how people can farm without them,' says Charles as he leans against his bakkie surveying the perfectly choreographed dance between dogs and sheep in the pastures.

By some strange karmic coincidence, the Lords had delivered their first batch of cheese to the well-known Daggaboer's Padstal just hours before Kobus Mulder happened to be passing through the area. He saw their cheese, tasted it, gave them a call, and arrived at their farm that same day. Karen, in true Eastern Karoo style, invited him to spend the night with the family, and Kobus has been a regular visitor since. 'This is the Karoo!' says Karen, smiling, 'people aren't strangers for long'.

Kobus's Cheese Notes

Homer was so impressed with sheep's milk cheese that he had the Cyclops make it in his *Odyssey*. I was equally impressed when I tasted the sheep's milk feta made by the Lords on Beaconsfield Farm. I had to travel 70 km on a gravel road to taste the first sheep's milk feta made in South Africa, but it was worth it. According to Greek mythology, the gods sent Apollo's son to teach the Greeks how to make cheese, and the first cheese that they made was feta. Today, the Beaconsfield sheep's milk feta is very close to the feta which the Greeks love in their spanakopita and many other dishes.

Because of the higher fat content of sheep's milk, Beaconsfield feta has a very creamy texture, and many mechanical openings, which makes for an easy crumble over a salad or savoury tart. Although feta has a long shelf life, do not expect a well-developed cheese flavour in this feta, as it is not matured for a long period. Apart from the well-balanced salty and slightly sour taste, it also has a distinct flavour, which comes from

Beaconsfield Gouda

Beaconsfield Feta

the grazing available to the Beaconsfield sheep. This flavour combination is just what one wants when using the cheese as an ingredient in salads or with cooked vegetables.

Another impressive Beaconsfield cheese is their halloumi. This popular cheese from Cyprus was originally made from the milk of the now-extinct Mouflon sheep. The dense and bouncy texture of Halloumi comes from the curd being kneaded in hot whey before being folded over like a wallet. In Cyprus, halloumi's salty and milky flavour goes well with fruits and vegetables, but elsewhere its high melting point has made it a firm favourite to enjoy fried or grilled as a warm, squeaky canapé or starter. Cypriot chefs insist that it should not be fried in any oil, as this seals the cheese and prevents the milk sugar escaping onto the rind. They claim that the heat causes the milk sugar to caramelise on the rind, giving it an unexpected sweetish flavour. I have to say that I agree with them.

Beaconsfield also produces sheep's milk Gouda and pecorino. All the types of cheese that they make are traditionally made with sheep's milk, but are often produced using cow's milk instead. Using sheep's milk dramatically improves the textures and the flavours of these cheeses.

Beaconsfield sell their products in Port Elizabeth, Knysna, Jeffreys Bay, Timberlake Village, George and other points along the Garden Route.

Beaconsfield Halloumi

Belnori

Bapsfontein, Gauteng
Norman & Rina Belcher

Situated on a smallholding in a black wattle plantation near Bapsfontein in East Gauteng lies the home of Norman and Rina Belcher, cheesemakers at the Belnori Boutique Cheesery. (The name is formed from the first few letters of Belcher, Norman and Rina.) Spending time here, surrounded by their enthusiastic mixed pack of dogs, it's easy to relax and forget that Johannesburg is so near.

Until 2002, Norman and Rina had no animals on their property. Then a friend gave them an unusual gift – a Saanen ram. They soon brought in some company for their ram in the form of four ewes, and in the same year five little ewes were born. By March the following year, the industrious Belchers were in business and selling their first goat's milk products from a small table at a morning market.

Most of their milking goats, referred to as 'the ladies', have been reared on the property, and enjoy an easy life. They roam in open paddocks during the day, and shelter in paved wattle huts. A healthy diet ensures milk of a high quality. A small herd of sheep, recently relocated from the Karoo, also now live on the Belchers' property.

When they ventured into cheesemaking, Norman and Rina immediately attracted praise for their semi-hard cheeses. As their confidence grew, they began to experiment with different varieties. Demand for Belnori cheese soared, and more milk was needed, but more milk always means more goats. Norman built more goat pens to accommodate the growing herd, incorporating a maternity ward, kindergarten area and a separate

area for the rams, known as Ramsgate. The herd grew steadily, as did the Belnori range of cheeses, which improved in quality with every batch.

They began the business in 2003, and have become one of the country's leaders in goat's milk products. Since 2004, Belnori cheeses have regularly won top positions at the South African Dairy Championships, and have fared well at the World Cheese Awards. The Slow Food movement has also recognised Belnori cheeses.

The names of Belnori's cheeses all have the suffix '-wood', taken from the smallholding's thick black wattles. Cheeses like Tanglewood, Driftwood and Mulderswood are always popular in the area. Mulderswood is a culinary nod to Mr Cheese himself, Kobus Mulder. Norman and Rina realised how much Kobus had contributed to their cheesery, and honoured his valuable input with this green peppercorn-flavoured cheese.

Apart from the distinctive names, Belnori cheeses are also known for their distinctive look. Rina half-waxes the rounds of cheese and lets the warm wax dribble around the cheese. Always innovative, Norman and Rina make a successful team, and their tight-knit group of staff makes the cheesery even more homely.

Although it is a small cheesery, and produces about 25 kg of cheese per day, Belnori has an excellent reputation. Since the business began, cheese has become an all-consuming passion for the Belchers, and Rina is active in promoting goat's milk products in South Africa. Norman and Rina are keen to share their knowledge and drive the South African goat cheese industry forward.

Kobus's Cheese Notes

The first time I visited the Belchers, I was presented with a number of perfectly shaped semi-hard cheeses. This is not the easiest type of cheese to start out with. Although their cheese had not been perfected at that point, that first tasting around the kitchen table made me realise the huge potential of these two enthusiastic newcomers to the world of artisanal cheesemaking. One of the original semi-hard cheeses, and one which we tasted that evening, was the Tanglewood. It is their best-selling cheese to date, and has a large and loyal following. During the manufacturing process, the curd is washed to reduce the level of lactose in the whey, a step that gives the cheese a mild flavour and softer texture, which cheese lovers adore. It is a versatile cheese and will give flavour and colour to a cheese platter or texture to any dish when used as an ingredient.

The Belchers began experimenting with other cheeses and soon began selling feta, made more exotic thanks to just the right quantity of dried olives and fresh rosemary.

As they expanded their business, their cheese got better all the time. Belnori cheeses have regularly won South African Champion titles at the annual South African Dairy Championships, and have received medals at the World Cheese Awards in the UK. When their feta with Greek herbs was awarded the coveted Qualité Award in 2007, everybody sat up and took notice of the energetic Norman and Rina Belcher. The following year the Belchers became advocates for an organisation of goat's milk cheesemakers. Rina became its first secretary, and driving force, in 2009.

In 2010, the couple stunned me with a white-mould cheese called St Catherine. Never before have I had the pleasure of eating a cheese with such a smooth and creamy texture and complex flavour. The white pâte, with an even whiter layer of mould on the surface, looks beautiful and did not disappoint when the first slice found its way into my mouth. I struggled to pinpoint the flavour, and still find it difficult to describe. It did not have the fermented flavour that is so often found in white mould, nor the ammoniac whiff that is so prevalent in well-matured white moulds. Everyone should find a St Catherine and enjoy its velvety texture and luscious meaty flavour.

In 2011, the Belchers brought in a flock of milking sheep from the Karoo. Norman and Rina wanted to try their hand at sheep's milk cheese, and soon produced two stunning cheeses, at either end of the cheese spectrum. Serengeti is a semi-hard cheese with a melt-in-the-mouth texture and a true umami flavour. This one-kilogram round cheese is destined for big things, and I will watch its trophy life with great interest. Their other sheep's milk cheese, the softer, smoother, white-mould Sonata, is one of those cheeses that touched the tip of my tongue at the right time. This little cheese, which I smuggled in my hand luggage to participate in the 2011 World Cheese Awards in Birmingham, charms everyone who comes across it. The panel of French judges were so seduced that they awarded it a Gold Medal. It doesn't surprise me that Grand Maître Roland Barthélemy closed his eyes with pleasure when he first tasted it. He could not believe that this little teenage cheese, looking like a fluffy cloud, could create such a flavour explosion in his mouth.

Belnori Gypsy King

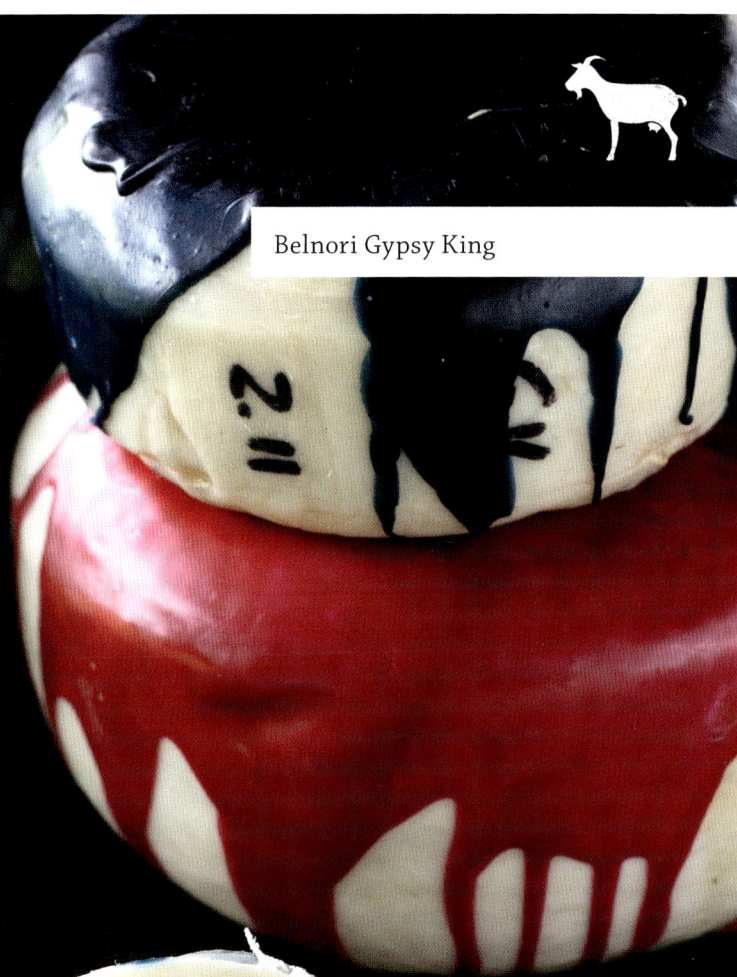

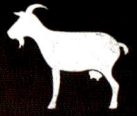

Belnori Phantom Forest

Belnori Mulderswood

Buffalo Ridge Mozzarella

Wellington, Western Cape
Wayne Rademeyer

A few kilometres outside Wellington in the Boland, a herd of water buffalo graze peacefully on the banks of the Berg River. The scene couldn't look more natural, but this is actually the only herd of water buffalo being farmed and milked in South Africa. To get his impressive herd to the farm was a labour of love for cheesemaker and farmer Wayne Rademeyer – a love for good mozzarella.

A few years ago, buffalo mozzarella was unobtainable in South Africa, and the only option was to import it from Italy. 'While I appreciate what the Italians did', explains Wayne, 'there is no reason why we can't replicate it here. It is not feasible to import everything, so why not make it locally?' He is determined to banish the idea of mozzarella that so many South Africans have. 'Mozzarella has a flavour, but so many people think it just tastes like that plastic, rubbery white stuff that you find in supermarkets.'

Wayne's desire to provide South Africa with world-standard buffalo mozzarella required a farm, a knowledge of cheesemaking and a herd of riverine water buffalo. He realised the challenges facing him, but was determined to succeed. It took him six years to find the animals he needed, and another two years to import them. He now knows each buffalo by name, and can even tell the birth dates of each animal. The first South African calf was born on 27 July 2007. Many of his bulls are named after famous Mediterranean lovers, like Don Juan and Casanova. 'I like to think that their names will inspire their behaviour during mating season,' he quips.

It soon becomes clear that Wayne likes to do things properly. He wanted to make buffalo mozzarella, and would not settle for anything less. 'It's not worth using any mozzarella other than buffalo, and it must be done properly', he explains. Wayne comes from a legal background and is a self-taught farmer, or as he likes to put it, 'a Google farmer'. 'I'm still learning,' he chuckles as he inspects his herd in the morning. He bought a farm, left Johannesburg, and changed his lifestyle from the fast-paced business world of the city to the slower, tougher life of a farmer in the Boland.

Buffalo Ridge Farm is kept as natural as possible to encourage wildlife and indigenous plant growth. No pesticides or chemicals are used, and although the farm is not yet certified, Wayne follows organic farming principles. These are evident throughout the running of the farm, from milking processes to farming practices. The buffalo are grass-fed, and Wayne's pasture consists of lucerne, clover and rye grass. Wayne's belief in sustainability extends to his workers, who are long-term employees (unlike many local farms, which hire workers on short-term contracts).

Kobus's Cheese Notes

The monks of San Lorenzo in Capua used to enjoy *mozzarella di bufala* as far back as the 13th century, but South African cheese lovers had to wait for Wayne Rademeyer before they could sample their own local buffalo mozzarella. The cheese belongs to the stretched curd type of cheese, known as *pasta filata*, and is often mistaken for *fior de latte*, which is mozzarella made from cow's milk. Due to appellation control rules, any buffalo mozzarella produced outside the Campania region of Italy cannot be named the original Mozzarella di Bufala Campana, but rather Mozzarella di Bufala.

Wayne follows the traditional, centuries-old method to make his mozzarella, using only whole milk and selected cultures to obtain the desired flavour and texture. The rennet-coagulated milk is cut by hand, and walnut-sized curd pieces are left in the whey until the desired acidity has been reached and the curd has a plastic-like consistency. These signs indicate that the curd is ready to be submerged in very hot water to undergo the *pasta filata* process, which is so unique to stretched-curd cheeses. After this step, the hot cheese is shaped and allowed to cool in cold brine for a short while before being placed in the cold room.

Buffalo Ridge mozzarella is a stretched-curd cheese shaped in the typical round balls of very thin layers of moist cheese. When torn between the fingers it shows definite signs of layering, which is always an attribute of an excellent Mozzarella di Bufala. Wayne has perfected the pearl-white colour, silky texture and the mild, slightly sour taste that is so characteristic of this king of *pasta filata* cheeses.

The cheese is ready to eat within one or two days of being made, and is springy and elastic for its first ten to twelve hours, but as it matures it becomes softer and creamier. When the delicate cheese is sliced to be served with tomatoes, basil, olive oil and black pepper, it exudes a few drops of whey-like liquid, which further enhances the unique and delicate aroma of buffalo mozzarella. Although always a delight to eat on its own, buffalo mozzarella also gives wonderful texture to a light meal like a caprese salad.

At the moment, Wayne produces mozzarella, ricotta and fromage blanc (similar to a cream cheese or mascarpone). He also makes paneer, a South Asian fresh cheese traditionally made with buffalo milk, and is developing provolone. Buffalo Ridge produces about 600 balls of mozzarella daily, and Wayne sells his cheese to top-end restaurants and delicatessens, mainly in the Western Cape.

Buffalo Ridge Mozzarella

Chrissie's Country Cheese

Galtee More Farm, Richmond, Midlands, KwaZulu-Natal
Chrissie Briscoe

Chrissie Briscoe, proudly eccentric doyenne of the cheese world, makes some of the most interesting and unusual cheeses in the country. She and her husband Peter live on Galtee More Farm, near Richmond in KwaZulu-Natal, and farm sugar cane in addition to their small dairy, which is run by their son, Alan. Chrissie has been making cheese on her farm for over twenty years.

Chrissie makes cheese out of pure love; her cheeses are world class, and completely unique in South Africa. She has won numerous awards over the years, and is almost single-handedly responsible for bringing craft cheesemaking to South Africa. If the cheese fridge in the local supermarket is a barometer of local tastes, a huge difference over the last ten years becomes obvious. Previously, it would stock Gouda and Cheddar, but now there is an unbelievable array of interesting cheeses. There is no question that Chrissie has been a huge part of that change, and she is well respected by cheesemakers around the country.

Her operation is small, and doesn't use more than 300 litres of milk a day, but she insists that she doesn't want to grow bigger in order to sell more cheese. The 30 Ayrshire cows that are milked on the farm bring in as much milk as Chrissie needs.

Cheesemaking, for Chrissie, is in every sense a labour of love. She was born and raised in Kenya, near a cheese factory called Njoro Valley. As a young girl, Chrissie would often visit this well-known operation, run by Michael Wisdom, and she dreamed

of making cheese. She worked for a time at the Long Clawson Stilton factory in England, the oldest Stilton factory in the world.

Chrissie has a passion for traditional English cheeses, and is crazy about Stilton and Red Leicester. She has a reputation for making especially pungent cheeses, and she encourages mould growth on Stiltons and Leicesters, which she ages.

Chrissie has been recognised by the Slow Food movement in Bra, Italy, as an ambassador of cheesemaking. Chrissie loves her cheese, and her customers can't get enough of it either. Most Saturday mornings find Chrissie at the local Shongweni market, though several outlets in the area also stock her cheese, and it is occasionally available in the Western Cape too.

She comes from a family of artists and creatives, and Chrissie is always inventing new recipes and different ways to create cheese. Every batch is unique, because she is always playing with textures and colours. Not all experiments are successful, but Chrissie wouldn't do it any other way. Her Ayrdy is a staple table cheese, which she supplies to a large national retailer, and many of her cheeses are South African homages to their English forebears. Natal Beetroot, for example, is similar to a Red Leicester. She describes her Stiltons as Stilton-esque, because Stilton is a particularly English cheese, and is greatly influenced by the environment in which it is made. It is also a seasonal cheese, so Chrissie stockpiles it for Christmas, when it is traditionally consumed. One of her biggest cheeses is her Red Sage, which is made with beetroot wine and sage. Chrissie creates her own cultures, a malodorous business but one she swears by.

Chrissie is knowledgeable about everything that goes into cheesemaking, and her small production facility is of an extremely high standard. Her whey is not wasted, and is used as fertiliser. Her animals are all fed naturally, and rear their own calves on the farm. Chrissie uses the milk that is left over, and does not pasteurise the milk before making cheese.

Kobus's Cheese Notes

Chrissie Briscoe, cheesemaker extraordinaire, is a woman whose passion for cheese knows no bounds. Chrissie and Peter's home on Galtee More Farm near Eston is a shrine to cheesemaking. It is the best cheesemaking museum in the world – better than Monroe in Wisconsin, Alkmaar in the Netherlands and Poligny in Franche-Comté. You need Chrissie to walk you through it, though, as none of the items are labelled with their origin. From the kitchen to the dining room, to the spacious lounge, and down the passage to the bedrooms, no space is left untouched. Cheesemaking memorabilia is stacked from the floor halfway to the ceiling. There must be more than 15 beautiful Stilton glass and ceramic domes on the dining room table alone. Cheese moulds, presses, wrappers and vats – you name it and you will find it here, collected from all over the world.

I did not know Chrissie until the first National Cheese Festival, held in the cellar of Grande Provence wine farm, in Franschhoek, where she was exhibiting her unusual multicoloured cheeses. Their robust and rustic appearance was very impressive: the pâte of one was a deep red from colouring the curds with beetroot – a good natural colour to use because it is most stable in foods with a low water activity. The semi-hard cheese next to it was as green as sweet basil, only it was coloured with green sage. I decided to taste it, because Native Americans swear that green sage is good for hair growth. The cheese had a lovely buttery texture with a few mechanical holes caused by leftover whey, but was firm enough to cut into thin slices for a cheese platter. In 2004, when I took this green cheese to the World Cheese Awards in London's Pillar Hall, one of the senior Welsh judges was intrigued by it and argued that the cheesemaker must have read *Every Woman Her Own House-keeper*, written by John Perkins in 1796. When I found this historic book in the British Museum the next day, I was intrigued to discover that it described the making of green sage cheese.

Chrissie's cheeses have intriguing names, like the slightly more matured Nguni and the very popular Wookie Ayrby. She is a practical cheesemaker and understands that her cheeses must be able to withstand the KwaZulu-Natal temperatures and the distances they have to travel to various markets. Each of Chrissie's cheeses has its own unique farm-style flavour, yet is never insipid nor overpoweringly piquant. Although one can use this type of cheese as an ingredient in a dish, I have always thought of Chrissie's cheeses as showpieces on a cheese board, whether in a five-star North Coast hotel or a cottage in the Cape Winelands.

Chrissie's Ayrby

Cloud Cottage

Avontuur, Western Cape
Eva Dry

The hills surrounding the little Garden Route farm of Voog se Kraal are definitely alive with the sound of music. Here, Eva Dry makes her Cloud Cottage cheeses, the best known of which are chèvres. Even without the pure-white Saanen goats dotting the hillside, the place has a decidedly Alpine quality.

Eva runs a small herd of Saanen goats, as well as a couple of Jersey and Nguni cattle. Each of the goats has a name, and, in the early evenings, Eva's voice is heard in the grazing pastures calling out their names: 'Peach! Rocket! Nutmeg! Kom, kom, kom! Quincey! Biffer! Cinnamon!'

Saanen goats, although often called 'Swiss', actually originated in North Africa. Eva loves their nature and the alert way they interact with the world. The tiny milking shed can handle eight goats at a time. While four are being milked by the vacuum machine, another four are led in and prepared for milking. Amazingly, they go to predetermined milking stations without being told or cajoled. Above each stall is a list with the names of three or four goats. Eva opens the door to the dairy, and calls four names. Four goats come in, go to the stall where their name appears, eat a treat and get milked.

While Eva is primarily in charge of the cheesemaking, her husband Chris manages the sales and marketing side. He is a regular stallholder at the popular Harkerville market on the N2 highway on Saturday mornings, where he sells cheese, and occasionally pork and vegetables. Eva is assisted in the dairy and in the cheesery by Rachel and Mantoor Desember, who have been gradually trained to take up more and more responsibility for this side of the farm.

The Drys' 800-ha farm is run on the principles of biodynamic and organic agriculture, which aims to unite ecological farming systems with sustainable ones. One of the central concepts of biodynamics is that the farm is an organism in itself, and the fewest possible external materials should be used. Because of this, Chris reckons that their cheese is healthier and tastes better in all its subtleties.

The farm uses virtually no electricity, except for the vacuum pump for the milking, which until recently required the use of a petrol generator. With a bit of tinkering and a lot of ingenuity, their eldest son, Benjamin, worked out a way to run the pump on hydro-gravitational power. Because their water source is some way up the hill from the dairy, and there are fields below the dairy to be irrigated, Benjamin calculated that they could harness the energy of the water to power the milking shed.

Another source of income for the farm is pork; the pigs are fattened on the leftover whey from the dairy. As the goats are milked, the warm milk flows into a tank where cheesemaking begins. As the curds form, the resulting whey flows in a pipe directly from the cheesery down to the pig sty in a lower paddock.

Eva's biodynamic vegetable garden is a vital part of the whole system. Not only does it provide greens and offcuts for the pigs, there are treats in there for the goats, and flavour inputs for the cheese as well. If any of the goats are sick, the first resort is herbs and medicinal plants from the garden rather than antibiotics. Then, of course, the animals provide material for the compost to fertilise the soil, and so the wheel turns.

It's a lovely cyclical process, and one that allows the family to eke out their simple existence. Despite the fact that they run a bustling little business, Eva does not like to dwell on such matters. 'We're not business-minded, nor are we competitive,' she laughs, 'we're farmers.'

Kobus's Cheese Notes

The uncomplicated Cloud Cottage goat's milk cheese, which Christopher and Eva Dry make high up in the Prince Alfred Pass between Plettenberg Bay and Avontuur, encapsulates all the attributes which they use to describe the farm: peace, tranquillity, mountains, rivers, sunsets and happiness. I met Chris and Eva Dry years ago when they first came up with the idea of producing a goat's cheese on their farm. Eva already had experience running a dairy and making cheese, but I thought their philosophy was very engaging. I like to call them the last true hippies in South Africa.

Despite the simplicity of their lifestyle and production process, the Drys produce exceptional cheese at Cloud Cottage. It has the signature of a truly excellent fresh goat cheese, with good depth of flavour. Rather than growing into a big business, they

keep production manageable, just big enough for their needs. Because you can't find it everywhere and you have to work a little to get it, Cloud Cottage cheeses stand out among local goat cheeses.

No two Cloud Cottage cheeses are ever quite the same. Simple processes allow you to discern the subtle differences. Their flavoured chèvres use ingredients they have grown themselves, which adds to the artisanal provenance of the cheese. They use natural cultures – one of the farm's very few external inputs – at the beginning of the season only. For the rest of the year, they make use of some of the curds held over from each previous cheese batch. This creates a unique environmental stamp on the cheese, as the culture is constantly being altered by its environment. In other words, it contributes to the terroir of the cheese.

In the eighth century, when the Saracens left the west of France, they left behind some goats and a method of making cheese using goat's milk. When I first visited Voog se Kraal, I truly believed I had found one of the last true followers of this method, balanced by simplicity and alchemy. The log-like *bûche chèvre* is a lactic-curd cheese, as used by every bistro in France to make the famous *salade de chèvre chaud*. Chèvre, the French word for goat, has become the generic name for this type of goat's milk cheese. Strictly speaking, only those made in France should be called this. However, and unsurprisingly, it is now applied to goat cheese made anywhere in the world.

Cloud Cottage makes the original natural type, but they also flavour some cheeses with herbs and peppers grown on the farm. The mild and creamy cheese, with its slightly acidic flavour, is ideal for a warm salad, but it is equally tasty on a cracker with some olives or figs. I like it best on a fresh bagel first thing in the morning. The somewhat crumbly texture spreads easily and looks more appetising than the icing-sugar appearance of most cream cheeses. And it makes any coffee taste better. The Cloud Cottage chèvre is regularly used in my home as a filling for omelettes and in soufflés – *très savoureux*.

Cloud Cottage also makes a cow's milk cheese in small quantities, but the lucky shoppers at the Garden Route morning markets, where Christopher sells their cheeses, are the few who get to enjoy this. Eva is currently experimenting with a new cheese, but, lest I say too much, I know it will be as good as their chèvre range. Cloud Cottage also produces Mouse Cheese, a unique aged chèvre with a very strong, sharp flavour.

Contented animals and happy cheesemakers are always responsible for lovely cheeses.

Cloud Cottage Chevin

Cloud Cottage Chevin

Cloud Cottage Mouse Cheese

Dalewood Fromage

Simondium, Western Cape
Rob Visser

In the heart of the Cape Winelands, along the scenic Franschhoek–Simondium road, lies a magnificent farm that is home to Rob and Petrina Visser and their herd of fine stud Jersey cattle. Surrounded on all sides by vineyards and wine estates, Dalewood Farm is making a real name for South African cheese. Rob's cheese has captured the tastebuds of connoisseurs around the world, and he and Petrina are proving themselves to be an astute business team, with exactly the right combination of business savvy and dairy experience.

Rob's father was a dairy farmer, and Rob is the second generation of Vissers to farm at Dalewood. 'I grew up a farmer', he says with gentle smile as he stoops his tall frame into the dairy. While studying dairy technology under the renowned South African dairy technologist Norman Robertson, Rob realised that he wanted to do something with the dairy that would really add value to the milk. After completing his studies, Rob spent some time in France, and saw a gap in the market. 'Cheese was something that South Africa needed,' he explains, 'but cheesemaking also just tickled my fancy.' He returned to South Africa with his head full of ideas, and married Petrina, who at the time was working in the wine marketing industry. She loved his ideas about cheesemaking and thought it would be a wise business decision. 'Petrina is all of the business acumen and marketing drive here!' Rob laughs.

The family's Jersey herd is the very picture of health. Fawn-coloured cows with soft coats and long eyelashes graze comfortably in the lush pastures. As a splendid young

cow swishes her tail and surveys the pastures through her thick black eyelashes, it isn't hard to believe she knows she is partly responsible for the delicious cheeses that are produced at Dalewood.

In 2002, Rob really began to devote himself to cheesemaking. With the support of Petrina, Rob began dreaming up the Huguenot. 'I was so inspired by all of the wonderful cheeses that I had seen in Europe,' he says. 'I liked the area-boundedness of French cheese, and wanted to create an equivalent South African cheese from this area.' Just as winemakers speak of terroir, cheese is the product of the milk, which is in turn a product of the environment in which it was made. So many aspects need to be taken into account, such as the climate and the diet of the cows, not to mention the environment in which the cheese is matured. There are an infinite number of factors that determine what a cheese will ultimately taste like, something that is commonly misunderstood.

Huguenot, the flagship cheese of Dalewood Fromage, has received accolades from all around the world. Rob Visser developed the cheese, and although there are flavours evocative of other cheeses, it is a completely unique and proudly South African product. It is currently the largest head of cheese being produced in the country, and is matured for a minimum of six months.

Once Rob had perfected the recipe for the Huguenot, it took about six years for the cheese to find its place in the market. Today, it is one of the most sought-after cheeses in the country. Rob proudly describes it as 'a cheese that stands alone'. It is one of the most highly awarded cheeses in South Africa, and has received major accolades around the world. Some of the many awards it has received have been at the South African Dairy Championships, the Slow Food Convivium and the World Cheese Awards. Importantly, it is a specifically South African cheese. It can be described as something between an Abondance and a Beaufort.

About 120 Jersey cows are milked daily at Dalewood, and the milk is pasteurised before the cheesemaking begins. The farm has an eco-friendly approach to grazing, and the Jerseys are grazed rotationally, spending each day on a green pasture. These pastures are carefully managed, beginning with the nurturing of the biological life in the soil, and they are not artificially enhanced in any way – no chemical fertilisers, insecticides or weed killers are used.

Rob and Petrina know that they are producing cheese of exceptional quality. 'The bottom line,' says Petrina, 'is that our cows are happy, and happy cows produce valuable, delicious milk, which in turn makes good cheese.'

Kobus's Cheese Notes

Until 2004, South African cheese lovers were under the impression that good brushed-rind cheeses, with their unmistakeably rich sweetness, could only be made from the milk of Abondance and Montbiliard cows, and one had to travel to the French Alps to enjoy these. Then Rob and Petrina Visser from Dalewood Fromage launched their Huguenot cheese, made from Jersey milk. That year I tasted their very first Huguenot, and I was stunned by its complexity and quality. The Vissers succeeded in making a truly unique South African cheese. Dalewood Fromage has managed to make their Huguenot as flavourful as the brushed-rind cheeses from the Rhône-Alpes region, but without the help of the wild herbs and flowers which the French have in abundance.

Dalewood's cows are pasture-fed, which is unique in South Africa for producers of Brie and Camembert. The cows' diet is carefully monitored, which ensures that the milk will have the optimal butter fat content – ideal for their cheeses.

The Huguenot is currently the largest head of cheese produced in South Africa, and is retailed at six and twelve months matured. The six-month matured Huguenot is firm but not as hard as the limited-release twelve-month matured, and quite literally melts in the mouth. Its rich, almost sweet, complex flavour has won it many fans and chef admirers. The twelve-month matured Huguenot has, apart from its aromatic caramel notes, a long savoury flavour, thanks to the attention it gets in the maturation cellar.

During its first few months of maturation, the Huguenot is brushed with salt water, which contains friendly micro-flora. This method is most similar to the French style. Dalewood's maturation process, or affinage, also follows the French process, and doesn't fast-track anything, uses no plastics, and relies on a certain amount of oxygen. Apart from the rich Jersey milk and artisan manufacturing method, it is this brushing that is responsible for the Huguenot's unique flavour. To date, the Huguenot's finest moment came in 2010 when it was awarded a Super Gold Medal at the World Cheese Awards in Birmingham, England. In cheese lover's language, this means that it was judged one of the twelve best cheeses in the world.

Camembert & Brie

Dalewood's Camembert is made in different styles and sizes, and their wide range of Brie comes with several carefully selected additives, such as green figs and wild mushrooms. My favourite is the Wineland Brie (currently Dalewood's biggest production) because of its creamy texture. It will always remind me of the very first Brie I ate, in a small bistro in Saint-Lô, Normandy. Full of earthy and mushroom

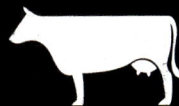

Dalewood Brie Superlatif

Dalewood Wineland Chef's Camembert

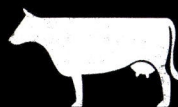

flavour, Wineland Brie shows a total absence of any ammoniac or bitter taste. It is an honest cheese that reflects the passion of Rob Visser and his team. It is made along traditional lines, where the coagulum is never cut, but rather ladled with three scoops into the moulds to ensure a perfect texture in the final cheese.

Dalewood also produces a Wineland Blue Camembert and Wineland Blue Brie, where the soft cheeses are interrupted with small patches of blue mould, which marbles the cheese beautifully and imparts an unmistakeable blue cheese flavour.

Rob and Petrina have dedicated agents around the country selling their cheese. Restaurants and hotels are regular buyers, and Dalewood cheese is also sold in Namibia, Mozambique and Mauritius. They also supply selected major supermarkets. In this way, they are well represented, and are not dependent on certain markets.

Another French classic has recently left the Dalewood stable, or rather the maturation cellar. It is a glorious washed-rind cheese whose aroma jumps into one's nose. The Languedoc is destined to cause a gastronomic sensation among cheese lovers who understand this style of cheese.

Petrina et Rob, j'aime vos fromages!

Dalewood Huguenot

Foxenburg Estate

Wellington, Western Cape
Marianne Hemmes

A short drive outside Wellington in the Cape Winelands lies the spectacular Foxenburg Estate, idyllically situated on the northern slopes of the Groenberg Mountain. In 1708 Simon van der Stel granted this pristine land to Johann Vosloo from Westphalia, Germany. It was originally named Vossenhof, and later renamed Foxenburg Estate. In April 2000, Marianne Hemmes and her husband Jan bought the beautiful property, and have worked hard to turn it into a highly regarded organic farm. Jan and Marianne inherited 15 Saanen goats with the purchase of the farm, and the small herd has since grown to 120. In season, the females produce copious amounts of milk, which is processed in the small and spotless cheesemaking facility.

'The South African cheese industry has blossomed in the last few years. There has been a development and change in the palates of the population,' explains Marianne. 'People are much more accepting of new and interesting flavours than they used to be.' Being of Dutch descent, Marianne found it natural and easy to devote herself to the pleasures of traditional cheesemaking methods, but cheerfully admits it is a labour of love. She is ably assisted by her husband Jan and a team of competent and enthusiastic staff. Marianne is originally from Cape Town, where she worked for years as a nursing sister, but trained at a Cordon Bleu college when she was young. Her background in food helped her to develop several of her own types of cheese, which have become very popular locally and won several awards.

Marianne's experience in the food industry has given her a good understanding of recipes and flavours, and her background in nursing gives her more insight into

Foxenburg Crottin

animal husbandry. Thanks to these influences, Marianne has proved an incredibly astute cheesemaker, and has developed an extensive range of handcrafted cheeses. Those uninitiated to the joys of goat's milk table cheese will be amazed to discover perfectly textured traditional favourites like Gouda and a Cheddar-style cheese.

All the Foxenburg cheeses and yoghurts are made using only 100% whole goat's milk, free of preservatives, hormones, antibiotics or colourants. The cheese gets a distinctive flavour from the goats' diet, which is determined by the terroir of the organic estate. The distinctive flavour of the products is not only influenced by the perfect pastoral mountain terroir that the goats inhabit, but also that they live and browse on certified organic pastures. Foxenburg is a certified organic farm, and also produces extra virgin olive oil, table olives and oyster mushrooms. The goats are milked early in the morning, and before cheesemaking begins the milk is pasteurised.

Marianne makes several hard and soft cheeses. A popular hard cheese is the Crottin, which is matured for two to three weeks and has a crumbly texture. Other hard cheeses include the Shepherd, the Foxtail (which is also made in a green peppercorn variety) and the Caprino Romano. Marianne developed the award-winning Shepherd and Foxtail cheeses herself, which are both mature hard cheeses (three to four months matured). Soft cheeses include chèvre, Chabris and cream cheese. The Chabris is a creamy and smooth cheese which is moulded into dome shapes.

In keeping with their conservation ethics as dedicated custodians of our rare natural heritage, Marianne and Jan have declared the greater part of the farm a nature reserve, and the area's rich biodiversity of flora and fauna is under the stewardship of CapeNature. As ardent members of the Renosterveld Conservancy, the tract of Groenberg on which Foxenburg is situated forms part of South Africa's largest intact tract of true unspoilt renosterveld.

Kobus's Cheese Notes

Foxenburg is not just any old farm. Not only is it part of the largest renosterveld conservancy in the Western Cape and a priority biodiversity site in the Cape Floristic Region, it boasts unequalled views from the verandas of its comfortable guest cottages. All this splendour goes well with the wonderful produce from the farm: meaty and robustly flavoured oyster mushrooms; peppery organic extra virgin olive oil obtained by picking and cold pressing on the same day; olives; apple cider; and, of course, the goat's milk cheeses.

The Foxenburg Saanen goats are lucky to be able to forage in the mountain terroir, which gives their milk and the cheese a unique and distinctive flavour. Marianne makes a well-balanced basket of fresh, soft and matured cheeses to satisfy the tastes of her many clients at the morning markets and delicatessens where her cheeses are sold. The conical soft Chabris is a favourite of mine, thanks to a mild and fresh acidic flavour that never overpowers the food it compliments. The brittle texture is delicate but sliceable and Chabris can be successfully used as a flavour-enhancing accompaniment. Marianne's matured cheeses are all excellent examples of her cheesemaking ability, and it is always difficult for me to identify a favourite. The Caprino Romano is an outstanding grating cheese, with a typical hard texture and a flavour profile that reminds me of the hard goat's cheeses of the Haute-Savoie.

Foxenburg Estate also produces exceptional hard cheeses like the Foxtail and the Shepherd. On a number of occasions, the judges at the South African Dairy Championships have crowned the Shepherd as South African Champion, and it has even won a Qualité Award, the prize sought by every cheesemaker in South Africa.

Jan and Marianne Hemmes have created a paradise of fine cheeses and food halfway up a Boland mountain. A French cheesemaker who once accompanied me to Foxenburg Estate summed it up best when he whispered absentmindedly to himself: *'exceptionnel'*.

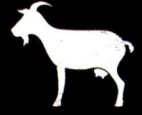

Foxenburg Queso Blanco

Foxenburg Foxtail

Foxenburg Farmhouse

Ganzvlei

Knysna, Western Cape
Chris Metelerkamp

Just outside the town of Knysna, situated on fertile fields along the banks of the Goukamma River, lies picturesque Ganzvlei Farm, home to the Metelerkamp family. Each morning, before dawn, there is a clatter at the old farmhouse as Chris Metelerkamp pulls on his gumboots, ready for a day's work. Chris Metelerkamp joined his father on Ganzvlei a little over thirty years ago, where they established a herd of pedigree Jersey cows. He always dreamed of adding value to the farm's production by making cheese, and with no more than 40 ha of good grazing, it was increasingly difficult to stay in the competitive dairy market. Although he also keeps a herd of Angus beef cattle, Chris was determined to produce a quality dairy product from his Jersey herd.

Chris began production in 2003. His decision to focus on making a mature Cheddar was driven by several factors; experience in milk retailing encouraged him to pursue a product with a long shelf life, but more important was his love of a good Cheddar.

Cheddar is a highly versatile cheese, which is one of the reasons why Chris likes it. He laughs, remembering the first disastrous attempts: 'There is nothing that can replace trial and error when it comes to actually making a consistent product.' Today, Ganzvlei produces about 500 kg of its unique and flavourful cheddar, Vastrap, each month.

The obvious problem with producing a cheese that needs such a long maturation time (Chris allows his to mature for a minimum of twelve months) lies in the wait between production and sale. This led Chris to experiment with cheeses that have a faster turnover. Again, Chris appealed to his own palate, and the result was Ganzvlei

Goukambert, a traditional French Camembert. With only six weeks to mature, the Camembert has proved the ideal cheese to supplement the Cheddar. The Camembert, Chris confesses, has been tricky to get consistent, which is also due to the fact that the two cheeses need to mature in slightly different conditions. The Camembert's mould needs to grow at a slightly warmer temperature.

Chris is passionate about cheese and making cheese: 'Cheese is a living process. What I like about cheesemaking is that it's a very simple and an organic process – I just let the bacteria do the work.' As he describes the process, he is hard at work over the cheese vat cutting the curds and draining the whey – intensive labour, but something that he does on most days. 'The curds and whey are full of life,' he adds, bending over the vat and working vigorously.

He is sometimes asked why, if no colourant is used, his Cheddar is not white. The answer lies in the milk of Jersey cows, which gives the cheese a natural creamy yellow colour. He tries to keep things as pure and natural as possible, and to make sure that there is a turnaround of nutrients on the farm.

Chris currently milks twenty cows a day, each yielding about 16 litres of milk daily. The cows are mostly pasture-fed, although they also get a small amount of meal supplementation. Jersey milk is high in both fat and protein, promoting a relatively high yield of cheese. Because Chris uses raw milk, subtle flavours emerge in the cheese that aren't noticeable in most cheeses made with pasteurised milk.

Cheesemaking truly is a science, and Chris has mastered the art of making an excellent cheese. The mature cheddar he creates speaks of long hours of careful labour, and it is clear that the Metelerkamps are wholly committed to making a world-class product.

Kobus's Cheese Notes

Ganzvlei Farm is situated in one of the most picturesque areas of the Garden Route. Chris Metelerkamp, farmer, cheesemaker and yachtsman, lives in harmony with the natural beauty, and this is reflected in his rustic cheeses.

The name of Chris's Cheddar, Ganzvlei Vastrap, was inspired by a painting, *The Foxtrot*, by Pierre-Auguste Renoir. Chris's artist wife Jenny agrees that it is apt for the cheese to be named for an artist who has inspired much of her own work. The Afrikaans word *vastrap* actually has a meaning that goes beyond the dance, and one which is very applicable to Ganzvlei: it translates as 'take courage and keep going'.

The Ganzvlei Vastrap has received an award from the Slow Food movement, an honour for which Chris is very proud, as 'slow food' encompasses the values he strives to maintain. With its earthy and unpretentious flavour, the cheese is a firm favourite with the foodies who flock to the weekly fresh food market in neighbouring Sedgefield. He mixes the evening and morning milk from his Jersey cows to make Vastrap, a true farmhouse Cheddar as defined by the rules applicable in the West Country of England, and slightly adapted to meet his practicalities. Vastrap matured Cheddar is made from unpasteurised full-cream milk in a 3 kg truckle, and is matured for six to twelve months, before being dipped in black wax. The cheese contains no colourants and, apart from a little sea salt, no preservatives. Ganzvlei cheese uses a bacterial starter and microbial rennet.

Chris is up and working in the dairy by 3:30 every morning, and the cheesemaking process begins immediately after milking. Most of Ganzvlei's cheese is sold at markets, but some is distributed to a number of cheese and fine food shops. The texture is not as dense and close as industrial Cheddar, and is a little more crumbly, which appeals to me when I enjoy it with white grapes and water biscuits. The earthy and robust flavour of the Vastrap makes it just the right kind of cheese for those who prefer matured Cheddar with a bite.

Chris also makes a soft white-mould cheese, which is like a full-cream Camembert-style cheese. It carries the interesting name of Goukambert, recalling both the Goukamma River, which runs through Ganzvlei Farm, as well as the cheese which inspired it. The creamy Jersey milk gives the Goukambert a deep colour, which alone makes my mouth water. It is covered in a smooth white layer of candidum mould, which helps to ripen the cheese from the outside. Left for four to five weeks, the cheese will become soft and runny throughout.

A cheesemaker must be a hardworking artist with scientific knowledge, patience and the ability to pay attention to the laws of nature. Chris Metelerkamp embodies all of these attributes, and makes honest, straightforward and utterly delicious cheese.

Ganzvlei Cheddar

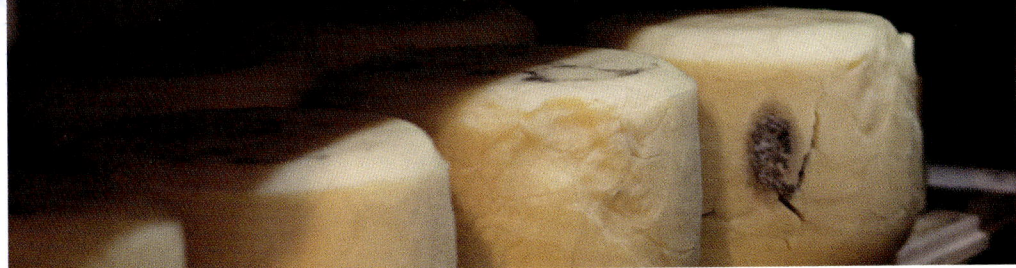

Ganzvlei Goukambert

Gay's Guernsey Dairy

Prince Albert, Western Cape
Gay van Hasselt

Church Street is the main artery of the little town of Prince Albert – 'the gateway to the Great Karoo' – at the foot of the Swartberg Pass. Along Church Street are beautiful old Karoo houses bordered by flowing lei water, charming coffee shops and antique stores; near the end of the road, as it rises towards the mountains, there is a small sign that announces 'Gay's Dairy'. If Church Street is the artery of the town, then Gay's Dairy is the heart.

Gay van Hasselt runs her business with a stern authority and twinkling bright blue eyes. She and her staff have a wonderful rapport, and, under her guidance, the dairy runs like a well-oiled engine. There is nothing about Gay's Dairy that is not done systematically and properly. Her herd is the top registered Guernsey herd in the country, and her cheeses have won numerous awards.

Every morning and afternoon, Prince Albert locals come to the dairy to buy cheese, milk and yoghurt. Restaurants and coffee shops around town feature Gay's products on their menus, and she also supplies the school and hospital. The dairy and the town rely on one another, and the small farm is integral to the town.

It is an extremely efficient dairy, but the peaceful and friendly atmosphere that prevails here seems to emanate from the cows themselves. As Gay says, 'I farm extensively and intensively. I run my lactating cows in town on the lands [about 15 ha] and the heifers and dry cows on the extensive Karoo property.' About 40 cows are milked each day, yielding approximately 500 litres of milk.

Gay employs several people to help with the cheesemaking, and all of the staff are local people who Gay has trained herself, empowering both herself and them. Christelene Kammies is integral to the operations of the dairy. She often oversees the cheese tasting, and knows all of the nuances to the cheesemaking processes. Christelene is the daughter of a woman who worked for Gay's family for years; Gay has helped her to get training in cheesemaking and dairy maintenance, and Christelene is now one of the country's award-winning cheesemakers.

Guernsey dairies are not common in South Africa, but there are good reasons for consuming Guernsey dairy products. Lactose intolerance is widespread in South Africa, but milk with the A2 protein – goat's milk is an example – does not affect those who are intolerant, even though it does contain lactose. Interestingly, about 96% of Guernsey cows have this protein in their milk, and Gay's products are often used by people who cannot consume regular lactose products. Scientifically, the A2 protein has been identified as containing the original form of beta casein produced by cows thousands of years ago. Beta casein represents a proportion of the protein content in cow's milk, and is made up of amino acids. The A1 protein is most commonly found in dairy cows today, and the theory is that this protein developed over time, through genetic mutation.

The story behind Gay's cheesemaking is not a romantic one, but one that small-scale farmers across the country can identify with. When asked how she started making cheese, and her answer is simple: 'debt'. She found herself in a situation where she had a major excess of milk, while the small and isolated town of Prince Albert did not provide enough of a market for milk and yoghurt. As with so many cheesemakers, Gay first started experimenting with feta, and laughs as she describes the first months of her cheesemaking. Her first batch of feta was made in an old cooler box, with plastic buckets serving as moulds.

Today, her operation is well equipped and smoothly run. An old round barn was converted to become the tasting and cooling room, and wooden shelves are piled high with the smooth wheels of cheese that have earned numerous awards for Gay.

Gay's Guernsey cattle are well adapted to the extreme conditions of the Karoo. In general, Guernseys are known for their adaptability to extreme and varying climatic and environmental conditions, and they thrive in environments in which other breeds would suffer. Gay's herd is one of the most productive and best managed in the country.

Gay is truly a force in Prince Albert. Everybody knows her, and visits from locals on quiet afternoons are common. People pass by the dairy to buy produce for the week and stay in her office chatting with Gay if she has the time.

Kobus's Cheese Notes

The most romantic way to Gay van Hasselt's Guernsey Dairy is through the beautiful Schoemanshoek farming area outside Oudtshoorn, over the spectacular Swartberg Pass, and into the town of Price Albert. Very few of the many visitors to Prince Albert do not stop at Gay's Dairy to taste and purchase some of her robust country cheeses. All of Gay's cheeses are made with unpasteurised milk, and are free of hormones, antibiotics, colouring, additives and preservatives.

Before Prince Albert became a popular place for city dwellers to escape to, Gay was already supplying the town with nutritious milk and yogurt from her Guernsey herd. Cows produce more milk in summer than in winter, and this meant Gay found herself with a surplus. But she made a plan, and soon was making feta in her kitchen, using pots and plastic buckets. The locals liked it and started demanding more, so Gay started producing a greater variety.

Trying her hand at traditional sweet-milk cheese, she discovered that although many of her customers liked the mild earthy flavour and slightly rubbery texture, many wanted a stronger cheese. While this first cheese, named Prince Albert Royal, sold well, Gay started experimenting with a more full-flavoured cheese; some months later, the Prince Albert Regal was ready for sale.

The Prince Albert Regal is a hard cheese with a low moisture content, which means that Gay could put a few on the top shelf to mature for a longer period and stronger flavour. When these were brought down for tasting after four months, they had developed a sharp and earthy flavour. So the younger version became the Prince Albert Regal Mild, and the more matured the Prince Albert Regal.

After local clients and restaurants again asked for more variety, and Gay's right-hand lady Christelene Kammies studied cheesemaking in France, a new cheese was born in the dairy. This time Gay took the royal bloodline to Italy and launched a grana-type cheese, appropriately named Parma Prince. This very hard grating cheese brings out the best of the raw milk that Gay uses for all her cheeses. The flavour is robust and lingers in the mouth if used as a table cheese. It is as an ingredient, though, that the this cheese attains its full potential. Its tangy taste and dry grainy texture lends a new dimension to pastas, and, in my opinion, it is the ideal cheese for a delicate soufflé.

Prince Albert Regal

Parma Prince

Goat Peter

Farm Waid, Magaliesberg Valley, Gauteng
Alastair Catto & Marianne Joos

Surrounded by thornveld, in the heart of the Cradle of Humankind in the Magaliesberg Valley, lies Alastair and Marianne's Farm Waid. They have been running Goat Peter, a small and successful cheesery, since 2008. Goat Peter was originally started by a Swiss couple who began their business with a goat named Heidi. Respecting the much-loved classic Swiss children's story, the company was named after Heidi's friend, the goatherd Peter. Although located far from the story's setting in the canton of Grison, high in the Swiss Alps, this South African cheesery makes world-class cheese. Since Alastair and Marianne took over the business, they have expanded the variety of cheese available from Goat Peter, and the quality has improved dramatically.

Marianne, originally from Switzerland, and her South African husband Alastair, make an excellent team. Alastair used to fly jets commercially, but goats are now his full-time passion. Alastair's love for his goats is unmistakeable when he talks about the finer details of goat farming and cheesemaking, and this passion is supported by Marianne's enthusiasm and quiet strength in their business. He began cheesemaking for medical reasons, after he was told that he needed to eat more live bacteria, which led to him making his own yoghurt.

The couple take particular pride in the fact that their cheese does not have the strong flavour that puts so many people off goat's cheese. Some people cannot tolerate the flavour of goat's milk products, and can recognise a 'goatiness' in cheese that others don't notice at all. Alastair and Marianne have paid particular to attention to this, and

Goat Peter Grison

there is no hint of pungent goat in their cheese. They achieve this through rigorous goat hygiene, and by keeping the ram separate from the does. Over a hundred goats are milked twice a day, and the milk is pasteurised immediately after milking. They make their cheese 'the old-fashioned way', keeping clear of preservatives and washing it with salt.

The couple is also strict about the goats' diet, which consists mainly of natural pasture and indigenous bush, all free of chemical fertilisers, and the goats have plenty of space to roam. A few years ago, the farm was home to 16 goats, but the herd has since expanded to 250. At first, they kept only Saanen goats, but Alpine Blacks and Toggenburgs have been recent additions. As the herd grows, the couple plan to use only the milk from the Toggenburg-Alpine mix in the future. In their opinion, the Toggenburgs are ideally suited to Farm Waid's climate.

Alastair and Marianne's products have been highly awarded in South Africa. In 2010, Goat Peter took the top honours at the South African Dairy Championships, and their cheeses were the first goat's milk products in history to win the top prize.

Kobus's Cheese Notes

Alastair and Marianne are immensely proud of their hard goat's milk cheese, which won the coveted Dairy Product of the Year title in 2010. However, their most popular cheese is halloumi. Customers love it because it is not too salty, and does not have the 'squeakiness' of many other halloumis.

Goat Peter's small and simple cheese was nameless until the evening of 28 April 2010, when news of the big prize reached Alastair and Marianne. They had always called it 'farm cheese', but they decided it needed a name, and christened it Grison, after the Swiss canton. This Sardo-type cheese has a firm to hard texture, which makes it great for soufflés and shaving over a green asparagus salad. The unique flavour is almost too complex to describe, which made the judges sit up and take notice. The flavour comes from the goats' diet and the cheesemaking techniques used by Marianne. It reminds me of a brushed-rind cheese made in the Swiss Alps, yet the rind is not brushed. With acid and salt in perfect balance, the Grison is altogether an unforgettable cheese.

Since that big day in 2010, Goat Peter's range has grown. Apart from the outstanding Grison and halloumi, Gouda, Cheddar, feta and delicate-tasting, fresh and soft bûchette-style cheese have been added. These delightful cheeses are available in many delicatessens and markets in the Gauteng region, and soon Alistair may decide to allow the rest of the country to enjoy them as well.

Goat Peter La Punt

Goat Peter Sils

Healey's Cheddar

Lourensford Wine Estate, Somerset West, Western Cape
James Healey

James Healey speaks passionately as he describes the processes and methods that he uses to make his exceptional mature farmhouse Cheddar. He began making cheese as a hobby many years ago, and honed his craft at the famous Montgomery's cheesery in Somerset, England. When he returned to South Africa, James was confident that he could make a good Cheddar.

He produced Healey's Farmhouse Cheddar in 2005. A year later he won the World Cheese Championships in the United States, and later that same year was awarded the prestigious Gold Medal at the World Cheese Awards in London. Healey has since garnered more awards.

James has a passion for the countryside and for good food. He strongly believes that 'the closer to nature the food is, the better it will be ... and the better it will taste too!' This belief is reflected in his choice of milk supplier – Elsenberg agricultural college, located outside Stellenbosch. The majority of the milk is from Friesian cattle, although about 15% of the milk is Jersey. James stresses the importance of the cows being pasture-fed on natural veld, because their milk produces very different cheese to cows that are grain-fed. There is a much higher percentage of butterfat, and the cheese also takes on a creamy yellow colour because of the chlorophyll in the grass.

Healey's Farmhouse Cheddar uses a cheddaring process that is unique in South Africa. 'No one touches the cheese as it's getting made in big commercial cheese factories', says Dennis Bean, the production manager, 'but our cheese is physically handled,

which is such an important aspect of cheesemaking'. Dennis has been working with James since the beginning of 2011, and comes from a background in finance – a rather different pursuit to producing handmade cheese.

Depending on weather conditions, plants, animals and people, there are subtle differences in flavour in each batch. 'If you are creating cheese in the traditional manner there will always be slight changes in flavour, because of the bacteria. I can see production change every day – a few seconds' difference there, different weather outside, the wind blowing ... and of course, different conditions that affect the cows, which results in the milk differing on a daily basis too,' says Dennis.

James and Dennis pride themselves on the way the cheese is made. Despite demand, they will never put cheese that is younger than eight months on the market. As with traditional farmhouse Cheddar in Somerset, Healey's produces 2.5-kg truckles and large 10-kg heads. James scratches his head as he points out the truckles, 'it's strange, a big head is never called a wheel, but the truckles are referred to as little wheels'.

Kobus's Cheese Notes

Who would have known, in AD 43, when Emperor Claudius invaded Britain, that the event would have such influence on the delicious Cheddar produced in Somerset West today? The invading Roman army included some cheesemakers, who soon taught the local tribes to make cheese. Today, Healey's Cheddar is still made in the very same way except for one difference – it is not matured for three years.

Not only does Healey's Cheddar have history behind it but also an intention to be the very best Cheddar available. The process starts with hygienically produced, unpasteurised milk, rich in the good bacteria so necessary to change the fresh curds into a magnificent cheese during its six to twelve months' maturation. The unique texture is achieved by 'cheddaring' the warm curds as soon as the desired firmness has been reached.

In the cave-like cold room, the heads of cheese are turned every day for the first six weeks of maturation, and thereafter less frequently. After six weeks of maturation, and again at three months, each batch is tasted and graded in order to determine the total maturation length.

Although milk quality and the manufacturing process play a large role in the making of this stunning cheddar, I believe the true secret of the flavour of Healey's Cheddar lies in the maturation process. Bound in cloth, the rind is soon covered with a thin layer of grey mould, which reduces moisture loss and allows the cheese to develop a

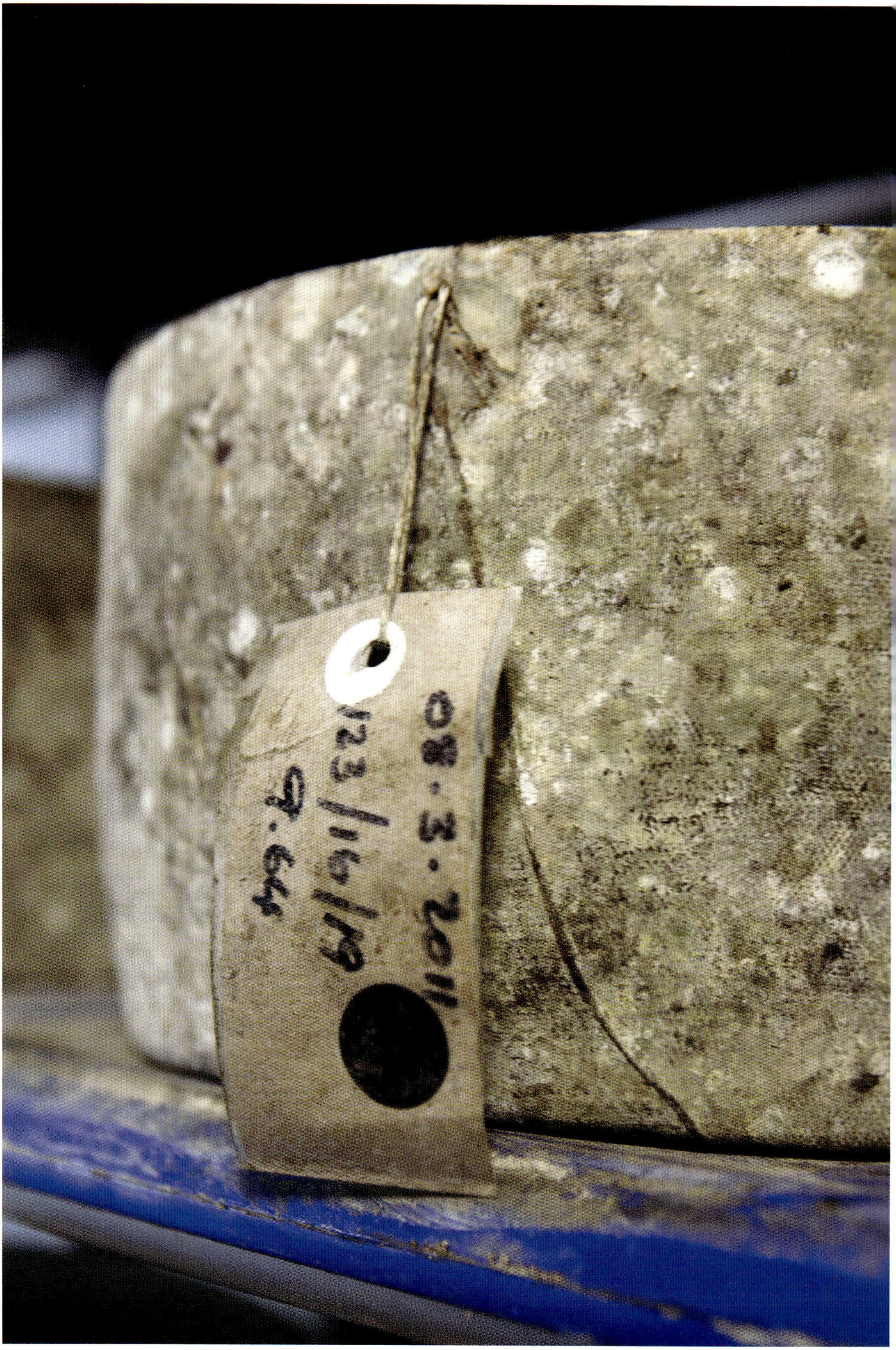
08.3.2011

dense texture and complex flavour. Through the ages, many cheesemakers have tried and failed to describe the typical Cheddar flavour, but Healey's Cheddar is even more difficult to define. The raw milk is responsible for a slightly earthy aroma, and the taste of six to nine months' matured cheddar will be a balanced mixture of clean acidity and savoury notes. The flavour of cheeses matured in excess of twelve months shows more sharpness, but the acidity, salt and proteolytic tastes are always in harmony.

Cheese is made four times a week at Healey's, with approximately 800 kg being turned out every week. The final product has a clean and nutty flavour and breaks easily, unlike many mass-produced cheddars, which bend. Cheddar is a versatile cheese and is equally good as a table or ingredient cheese. It almost feels wrong, though, to use Healey's Cheddar in a cheese sauce or grated over cauliflower. My call would be to savour every available crumb on my tongue, with my eyes closed.

Healey's Farmhouse Cheddar

Hijke Cheese

Doornkraal, Gauteng
Hester Hoogendijk

Doornkraal Farm is a beautiful smallholding located off the R25 outside Benoni. Here, Hester Hoogendijk runs a flourishing cheese business. She began Hijke Cheese in 1998, at first producing a variety of soft cheeses, but since 2003 has been manufacturing hard cheeses as well.

Hester started farming with cows in 1997. She started cheese production the following year, after attending a course and working in a small cheesery outside Pretoria for a few months. Today, she makes 20 varieties, which have won many awards and have plenty of loyal fans in the area.

Hijke Cheese is a family-run business. Hester's daughter-in-law, Kari, helps with the day-to-day operations. The cheesery team itself is like a small, happy family, and there is a lovely harmony in the factory. Kari's two young sons are often at work with her, and Hester happily spends time with her grandchildren when she is not working.

From a second-generation Dutch family, Hester makes cheese in the Dutch tradition, though her methods are a mix of traditional processes and new technologies. Hester's son, trained in medicine, is a technical genius, and it is thanks to him that Hester's cheesery boasts some of the best custom-made equipment in the country.

Hester always wanted to live on a farm, and geographically the 9 ha smallholding fitted into her plans. At first, she made cheese using milk from her own small dairy herd, which she later sold. She now buys milk in from a local Jersey cattle farmer so that she

Hijke Parmesan

can focus on the cheeses without the work of running a dairy. Hester emphasises that she doesn't just buy any milk; she and the farmer regularly discuss the cows' diet and Hester tests the milk for bacteria.

Kobus's Cheese Notes

I think of Hester Hoogendijk as one of the most entrepreneurial cheesemakers in the country. Before she began making cheese, Hester kept her own herd and sold milk to surrounding households. This didn't excite her business instinct enough, though, and she was sure she could add more value by making cheese.

A photograph of a cheese press has been displayed on the wall of my study for over ten years. This ingenious example of artistic engineering was built for Hester by one of her sons. With the help of her engineer husband and medical sons, a small cheesery was fitted out, and Hester began making cheese.

When I first met Hester, she was already making a very agreeable Gouda and a Cheddar which showed great potential. By that point she had learned about cheesemaking and had amassed practical experience. With her new-found familiarity, quality improved quickly, as did her range of cheeses. For reasons I can't explain, I have found that female cheesemakers seldom just make two or three cheeses; they want to make more varieties. Is it because they are so gifted and inquisitive? Perhaps it is to satisfy their own innovative minds. Hester is no exception, and she was soon making a wide range of cheeses, which included a Parmesan-type, a feta and a halloumi. In addition, her velvety Greek-style yoghurt flies off the shelves. The quality of her products is testimony to her skills and her understanding of milk microbiology and chemistry.

My personal favourites are Hester's pepato-style cheese and her Gouda Lite. I am not the greatest fan of cheese with additives, but the Hijke Pepato, a homage to the old Italian favourite, delighted me from my first taste. The close and dense texture allows for good slicing and grating, which makes it a perfect table and ingredient cheese. When it appears on my cheese platter during the summer, I enjoy it with Beurre Bosc pears and a wooded Chardonnay – a food trinity if ever there was one. The matured and distinct umami flavour of the cheese compliments the delicate pear, while the buttery Chardonnay cleans the mouth for the next portion. Hester matures her Hijke Pepato for six months, and I find this allows enough time for the fat globules and casein to break down. Many pepato cheeses are matured for too long, which brings out an off-putting lipase taste.

Hester's Gouda Lite is, simply put, just a Gouda cheese made from low-fat milk, but there is so much more involved in this wonderful cheese than just removing a bit of milk fat. Milk fat, unfortunately for the slimmers' community, plays a decisive role in cheese flavour. The reason why there are not more low-fat natural cheeses available in the world is because it is very difficult to produce a flavourful cheese from reduced-fat milk. Hester, however, defies this law, and is responsible for making a lower-fat cheese which delivers all the promise of a great cheese. By using specially selected cultures, she has placed a bigger emphasis on proteolysis, the process of breaking down the casein while the cheese is maturing for six weeks. The result is a mild but flavourful cheese, which is a great table and snack cheese. Its semi-hard texture allows thin slices to be cut for open sandwiches and snacks.

When rugby enthusiast friends visit and we watch a game together, I always serve Hijke Gouda Lite, dried apple rings and Hout Bay Sauvignon Blanc. They always look forward to watching games in my television den, and I often wonder why, as my equipment is old and the reception temperamental. It took me a whole rugby season to realise why they say my den is the best.

Hijke Gouda Lite

Indezi River

Midlands, KwaZulu-Natal
Wendy Harris & Barbara Robertshaw

Indezi River is one of the few cheesemaking operations in South Africa that produces both cow's and goat's milk cheeses. This family business, located at Balgowan in the heart of the Midlands, has become quite an institution in KwaZulu-Natal. In the rolling hills of the Midlands, Wendy Harris and daughter Barbara Robertshaw farm cows and goats, and run an extremely efficient cheese business. When driving up the dubious dirt road leading to the farm, it's easy to forget that the busy N3 highway is a short distance away.

Before they started Indezi, Wendy and Barbara were cheesemakers at another cheese factory, and between them have over twenty-five years of experience. One of the pioneers of artisanal cheesemaking in South Africa, Jimmy Harris, was an inspiration and teacher to both women.

Indezi has grown considerably over the years, but the farm has lost none of its charm. Wendy and Barbara employ and look after a large team of staff. There are people on the farm who have been working there for many years, and there is an unmistakeable family feeling to the place. They run a very efficient operation, keep their facilities spotlessly clean, and have been officially certified a free-range dairy.

There is a large variety of cheese available from Indezi River. Their cow's milk cheeses range from pecorino and smoked Cheddar to Kwela Kwela and Kwaito. Their goat's milk cheese includes the popular soft and creamy Calabash, available both plain and with additives, as well as feta and specialities like N'tabamhlope and Nandi. Barbara and

Wendy can also boast that they produce the only blended-milk cheeses in South Africa. They made the decision to pasteurise their milk before cheesemaking, and about 80% of the milk they use is from their Jersey cow and Saanen goat herds.

Kobus's Cheese Notes

Wendy Harris and Barbara Robertshaw already had fifteen years' cheesemaking experience behind them when they decided to start Indezi River Cheese. The artistic streak in Wendy Harris and the practical one in daughter Barbara made them the ideal team to start a new cheesery from scratch in 2002. The late Jimmy Harris, an engineer and pioneer artisan cheesemaker himself, completed the formidable team with his technical and strategic knowledge.

Known during the first years as goat's milk cheesemakers, they added cow's milk cheeses to their range, and today they make eight goat's and eight cow's cheeses. I suspect the arrival of son-in-law Paul Nash some years ago had something to do with this strategic step. Making and marketing 16 cheeses nationally is a huge task and responsibility, particularly when the cheeses are as divergent in character and style as the Indezi River range. Every cheese has its own method of manufacturing, which includes temperature, level of lactic acid development and, once made, maturation temperature, humidity and period.

It has taken me a long time to taste my way through this range, and I must admit that the ones with Zulu names remain my favourites. Indezi River was one of the leaders in giving their cheeses truly South African names, a step that their clients obviously liked. The Kwaito is a semi-hard cow's milk cheese made from full-cream Jersey milk, which becomes more apparent once you have it in your mouth. The mild and somewhat sweet flavour makes it ideal as a table cheese, although I have seen it used successfully to make a perfect sauce for asparagus. It also comes in a variety of additives, such as black pepper and herbs, but the plain one is my favourite. Nandi, which means 'sweet' but was named for a Zulu queen, is a stirred-curd hard goat's milk cheese. The texture is slightly open but it slices and grates easily, which makes it ideal as an ingredient to lend flavour and texture to a dish. No colourants are used in any of the Indezi River cheeses, so they contrast appetisingly with accompaniments on any cheese platter. However, if you want to see and eat a spectacular cheese, go for the Umcimbi. It consists of layers of cow's milk cheese on the top and bottom with a layer of goat's milk cheese with herbs in the middle – pure eye candy, but with a flavour explosion in the mouth. The texture is firm to hard, which makes slicing easy, and the flavour reminds me of a good British farmhouse cheese. Indezi River cheeses are versatile; they can be used as table cheese or ingredients in dishes for all the seasons of the year.

Indezi Kwaito

Indezi Umcimbi

Indezi Vinette

Indezi Calabash

Klein River

Stanford, Western Cape
Jacko van Beulen

A small cluster of buildings lies in the beautiful green Klein River valley, just outside the town of Stanford, nestling between the Kleinrivier mountains and the ocean. Winding down the muddy road towards the Kleinrivierskloof Farm, the hills sparkle with recent rainfall while the fresh smell of a cold ocean drifts over the hills. This is the home of Riaan and Shelley Lourens, who run Klein River Cheese with the help of their daughter, Sandy. Over the years, Klein River has grown from a simple dairy farm to one of the country's most successful cheese businesses.

The Stanford area is ideal for dairy farming as it experiences a mild climate, moderated by the cool, moist winds arriving from the ocean. Riaan inherited the farm from his father, Willem Lourens. However, by 1995 fluctuating prices made it more and more difficult to supply milk to big companies, so Riaan and Shelley began to look at value-enhancing alternatives for their milk. Riaan became interested in cheese through his friend Ken Borcherds, an elderly Hermanus cheese connoisseur, and, with his help, began experimenting. They started off by using the surplus milk from their own dairy. At that time, the South African cheese market was dismal, and Riaan and Shelley wanted to produce something different. 'All you could find in supermarkets that was locally made then was horrible plastic Cheddar and Gouda!' Shelley remembers.

Riaan had noticed the popularity of imported Gruyère, and that no one in South Africa was producing anything like the Swiss hard cheese. At first, Riaan and Shelley enlisted the help of Johannes Harslem, a Swiss-German cheesemaker, who helped them set up

their factory, and taught a local cheesemaker, Jacko van Beulen (who was then making blue cheese), the Swiss style of cheesemaking. In Jacko, they found a cheesemaker with experience, but who also showed a great deal of initiative and creativity. The relationship has proven fruitful, and now, nearly eighteen years later, Klein River is a successful cheese company, with Jacko the champion cheesemaker. His trademark cheese, the Van Beulen, has won several prizes.

In 2007 Riaan and Shelley ceased dairy production to focus solely on cheese. Now they get their milk delivered daily from four farmers in the area, and they pasteurise it on the farm. The milk is a combination of Ayrshire, Jersey (75%) and Friesland.

To date, Klein River has won numerous awards, both locally and internationally, and the cheese factory has grown significantly. With Jacko, Shelley and Riaan's energy and initiative the list of cheeses has grown considerably from the original Gruyère. Ten types of cheeses are produced, their styles ranging from Swiss and Danish to cheeses developed on the farm by Jacko. Klein River currently produces about ten tonnes of cheese per month, about 70% of it Gruyère. Over the past nine years Klein River Gruyère has outdone its Swiss rivals four times. At the prestigious World Cheese Awards in London several Klein River cheeses have been chosen as Qualité Outstanding Products, and they have received numerous awards at the South Africa Dairy Championships, as well as a Slow Food award for creativity and their pioneering efforts to extend the range of South African cheese.

Riaan travels to Europe to get inspiration from cheesemakers there, and comes back to South Africa to experiment. The commitment that the Lourens family has shown over the years adds to the value of Klein River Cheese. They have moved with the times, and adapted to new trends, exposing people to cheeses that they might never have sampled elsewhere. The years of experience do make a difference at Klein River Cheese, but it is the hard work, passion and inventiveness of Riaan, Jacko and Shelley that give its success true meaning.

Kobus's Cheese Notes

Like many South African dairy farmers in the 1980s, Riaan and Shelley Lourens decided to stop selling the quality milk of their Friesland herd to big milk buyers, and instead to add value to it themselves. The difference between them and many other dairy farmers is that they succeeded.

Their original South African-style Gruyère soon became a favourite, and cheese lovers started pressuring the couple for more varieties. Together with Jacko van Beulen they started experimenting with Havarti, Danbo, Leiden and Colby. Ten years down the road, and after cheesemaker Jacko trained in France, they developed a raclette and the unique Stanford and Van Beulen cheeses. These soon became popular due to their complex flavour profiles.

The South African Gruyère is sold at three, six and ten months, each with its own flavour and texture identity. The youngest cheese has the typical fruity-sweet flavour and dense texture that makes it an ideal snack cheese. The six-month matured cheese shows complexity in its flavour, with hints of tanginess and a more grainy texture, making it more versatile as a table and ingredient cheese. The ten- to twelve-month matured cheese is, with its crumbly texture and intensely strong flavour, the *pièce de résistance* of the trio. Although excellent with sourdough bread and a glass of Syrah, for me it shows its class when used in a soufflé.

The Stanford (named after the nearby Overberg town) is one of Klein River Cheese's own creations, and can be compared to a Gruyère. It is a flavourful cheese, matured for three months. Also unique to Klein River is the Van Beulen, a strong, dry cheese with a complex and unique flavour, matured for four and a half months.

Because of the popularity of the cheeses with the many tourists who visit the Walker Bay area, it was decided to add a farm shop to the cheesery. This modest outlet has grown considerably, selling the many different cheeses made by Klein River, as well as many other food items.

Pay Klein River Cheese a visit and taste the complete range of cheeses they make. You will be impressed by the pale and aromatic Danbo, with its elastic texture, which makes it my favourite cheese to enjoy on Capelli bread. The creamy Havarti, with its washed-rind flavour, will stun you with its luxurious mouth feel and smooth light texture. Try the raclette grilled on your favourite rye bread. This cheese, with its rich nutty and sweet flavour, is ideal to grill over boiled potatoes or blanched vegetables. Delicious!

Klein River Stanford

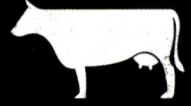

Klein River Raclette

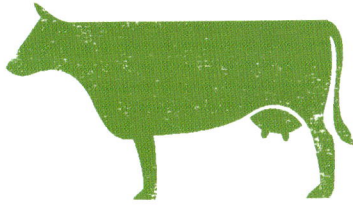

Myst Hill

Geelhoutboom, George, Western Cape
Ben de Villiers

Ben de Villiers has been living on his farm Myst Hill in the lush countryside of the Geelhoutboom area, outside George, for thirty-three years. He has farmed all his life, and grew up on a sheep farm in the Karoo. He moved into cattle farming when he moved to the George area.

He farms a mixture of cows, from Simmentaler to Jersey, and is not particular about the breed of cow whose milk he uses for making cheese. Ben has quite an alternative take on dairy farming, and doesn't believe in the common dairy farm practice of separating a calf from its mother shortly after birth.

He started making cheese about four years ago, but was already familiar with producing dairy products; he is the farmer behind the delicious Myst Hill butter, which so many chefs and deli owners swear by. After experimenting a little with cheese, Ben went on a short course in Plettenberg Bay, where he learnt the basics of cheesemaking. He has since taught himself a great deal through practice and seeking the advice of others. Although his butter production provides the bulk of his sales, demand for his cheese is quickly overtaking the 700 to 800 kg he produces each month.

Ben's speciality is Gouda, and he also makes a cumin variety. His cheese matures for at least six weeks before it goes on sale. Ben uses raw milk, as he believes it makes better cheese. The milk is all from his own cows, and he is confident about its quality. All farming processes are as natural as possible, which ensures that his milk is free of antibiotics and chemicals. His cows are pasture-fed, where they eat grass and legumes

Myst Hill Labneh

supplemented by a small amount of maize concentrate. He believes that this enhances the flavour of the milk and makes it creamier.

Kobus's Cheese Notes

Ben de Villiers was what I call a 'grass farmer', or, more correctly, a roll-on lawn supplier along the Garden Route, before an influx of competitors made him decide to do something else to compensate for lost market share. Although the George-Blanco area is one of the best milk-producing areas in South Africa, Ben and his son Mark cleverly farmed with dual-purpose Simmentaler cattle. They were selling milk to a local milk processor when Ben decided that he could add more value by trying his hand at cheesemaking. With the help of his wife, Shane, he scanned the internet and soon found an unused 200-litre cheese vat for sale. He quickly snapped it up and brought it to Myst Hill. With the help of some elementary cheesemaking books and the omnipotent internet, Ben set out to make 250-g baby Gouda cheeses using the traditional Dutch Boerenkaas method. These unpasteurised-milk cheeses were a hit from the start, and Ben was soon making cheese every day of the week. More cows came into lactation, and soon he was making his heavenly full-cream yogurt and delicious farm butter for clients along the Garden Route.

Ben makes cheese from milk that comes straight from the milking parlour, about 50 m away from his compact cheesery. Cheesemaking has become part of his daily life. The milk arrives around 7 am, and after stabilising it at 32 °C, he adds the microbial rennet and lets it do its work while he has breakfast. If I did not know that cheesemaking is hard work, I would say Ben is living a gentleman's life.

I am not sure which is more popular: Ben's cheese, his full-cream yogurt or his creamy-coloured butter. Each product has its own fans, but in my opinion the standout is his plain Gouda cheese, which lasts only three days in my household – less on weekends.

Myst Hill Gouda

Myst Hill Cream Cheese

Ovis Angelica

Smithfield, Free State
Elmarie van Aswegen

Elmarie van Aswegen does nothing by halves. The word 'maverick' comes to mind when thinking of this determined, tough and innovative woman. Elmarie is recognised as the pioneer of sheep's milk cheese in South Africa. Out of her vision and perseverance has come South Africa's first sheep's milk cheese company, Ovis Angelica (Latin for 'angelic sheep').

Sheep farming runs in Elmarie's blood. She lives on Patria, a 1 600-ha farm outside the Free State town of Smithfield, in one of South Africa's largest wool-producing districts where she is the sixth generation of Van Aswegens to farm sheep.

Elmarie, however, is the first Van Aswegen to milk her sheep. In fact, her sheep milking machines were the first of their kind to be installed in the country. In 2001, when she began milking, she was met with scepticism from local farmers and family alike. 'I had to develop a thick skin and learn to put my foot down,' she remarks wryly. 'If they hadn't been so difficult I wouldn't have been so determined to be a success.'

Ovis Angelica has won a Qualité Award for its best-known product, the Jan Groentjie, a fresh sheep's cheese made with dried lavender. Although humble about winning awards, Elmarie realises the value of her product, and advocates the nutritional value of sheep's milk products.

Elmarie milks up to 60 sheep a day throughout the year. Her sheep usually eat green fodder such as oats, but they also get a dry ration, which is a formula of lucerne, maize

and molasses. Elmarie is currently the sole South African breeder of the SA Milk Sheep. Although she calls her operation 'slightly rustic', Elmarie has adapted it to meet the strict standards of large retailers, and she runs a spotless outfit.

She is one of the few farmers in South Africa with permission to import dairy genetics. However, when she first tried to make arrangements to import genetics, she was told that a full biological impact study from a tertiary institution was needed. This had stopped many dairy farmers in the past, but Elmarie was unfazed. Instead of seeing it as an obstacle, she viewed it merely as a natural progression and decided to take it a step further. Instead of hiring someone to do the research and compile the report, Elmarie resolved to do it herself. She promptly enrolled at the University of the Free State and wrote the impact study. She has since received a Master's degree in Sustainable Agriculture.

Integrity in practice and behaviour is central to Elmarie's philosophy. She believes in being open with her clients, and associates a good product with a good life. Not only is all the cheese made by Elmarie, but she also oversees the farm administration and mutton and wool production. There is a strong spiritual angle to Elmarie's business, and for her 'the business has always been like a spiritual quest, and must be used for a higher purpose'.

Kobus's Cheese Notes

Like Hanne Nielsen, who gave Denmark Havarti cheese, and Marie Harel, who gave France Camembert, Elmarie found herself at a crossroads when she invented her cheese. As the sixth generation to farm on Patria, she had to think hard and deep about how to add value to the farm.

Almost two years later, she succeeded when she began making labneh (also known as yogurt cheese), an Eastern Mediterranean cheese used in sweet and savoury dishes or as a snack. Not only was sheep's milk cheese unknown in South Africa, but so were the little round balls of labneh. She soon followed with halloumi, a cheese that is slightly better known. However foreign the concept of sheep's milk cheese, customers did not need convincing because both cheeses were of such excellent quality.

During 2003, Elmarie made a new cheese that she called Jan Groentjie, the old Afrikaans name for the malachite sunbird (*Nectarinia famosa*). This soft, slightly salty, round little cheese is infused with organic lavender buds, which create a flavour explosion on the tongue. Although the lavender does impart a touch of sweetness, she didn't want her cheese to sound like a dessert. Jan Groentjie is ideal as a table cheese, but can also be used with success in pasta dishes. Elmarie describes its flavour as 'a blast of fresh air'. She is currently developing a new cheese, which combines Emmenthal cultures and Gouda processes.

Elmarie's cheeses contain no stabilisers, preservatives, colourants or any other chemicals. Most of her cheeses are those that traditionally should be made with sheep's milk, but nowadays are usually made with cow's millk.

The real king of cheeses in Elmarie's basket is the Pecora Africana. This pecorino-style cheese lends variety and taste to any cheese platter, and texture and flavour to any dish over which it is grated. Cheese lovers know that Italian pecorino is made from sheep's milk. I enjoy mine with Colombard grapes and two-day-old *pain de campagne* – aristocratic food.

Ovis Angelica Jan Groentjie

Ovis Angelica Ambrosia

Ovis Angelica Halloumi

Silver Lily

Geelhoutboom, George, Western Cape
Marianne Schroeder

In the rural outskirts of George, nestled in tranquil farmlands surrounded by the Outeniqua Mountains, Marianne Schroeder has created a lifestyle that perfectly suits her Dutch heritage. Here, on Silver Lily Farm, she makes typical Dutch cheese.

Before she moved to South Africa, Marianne lived for fourteen years on a 150-year-old wooden schooner in the Mediterranean. In the early 1980s, she and her late husband bought a small farm outside George and settled on the property, which they called Silver Lily. Making cheese was never part of Marianne's plan, but after two years she realised that there was very little variety of cheese available in South African shops and supermarkets, and so decided to start making her own. She went back to the Netherlands for a while to learn the basics.

Marianne's cheesemaking was at first a process of trial and error. She soon realised that she could not follow the exact processes that she had learned in the Netherlands, and would have to develop her own recipes, slightly adapted in order to meet South African constraints. Several years ago, Marianne was producing a much larger amount of cheese than today. 'I am not as young as I was, and now I am just doing it for myself,' she says with her subtle Dutch accent. Now she makes cheese on Tuesdays, and mostly supplies private clients.

Marianne uses only raw milk, and will strongly attest to the quality of cheese that results. 'Cheese made from raw, unpasteurised milk has a stronger flavour,' she explains. Big cheese companies generally buy from several dairies, and therefore

need to pasteurise their milk, but she buys milk from a farmer in George who has a Friesland dairy. Her choice of Friesland milk was deliberate, as traditional Dutch cheese is made primarily from this milk.

Her Dutch heritage influences much of Marianne's lifestyle – not just her cheese – and she arranged for a small *klompengolf* range to be set up on the farm. 'Nobody here really knows what it is,' she shrugs as she describes the golf sticks with clogs attached to their clubs, 'but the children love it.' This attitude is typical of Marianne: she does what makes her happy. With her gentle manner, it's difficult not to appreciate her efforts.

Marianne's operation is simple, and she employs two women who help with production on days that she needs them. Her equipment is not state of the art, but 'it's all I need'. She has devised her own ingenious way of pressing her cheese while it is in moulds, using simple wooden frames, string and weighted bottles.

Locals and tourists often come to visit the farm for a cheese tasting. Her small factory is a pleasure to visit; although it is small, it is kept in such meticulous condition that one wonders where she has time to make cheese in between all of the tidying. 'Maybe that's the Dutch in me!' she says.

Kobus's Cheese Notes

Marianne Schroeder loves Dutch cheese, so it's no surprise that she makes a Dutch-style cheese. Her cheesemaking is as close to the Dutch Boerenkaas method as you can get in South Africa, and her cheeses reflect the traditional style and taste. Some years ago, she made only traditional young and matured sweet-milk (Gouda) cheeses, but now produces a wider range of innovative cheeses. She waxes each head carefully after the brine has dried, and meticulously layers each four times, waiting for the layers to dry in between.

Marianne's Caserio is her own innovation, but its Gouda-style texture indicates its Boerenkaas heritage. The slightly acidic taste, however, shows that the curd was not washed to the same extent as real sweet-milk cheese. The Caserio comes in a range of popular flavours, including mustard seed, Mexican mix and smoked. These cheeses add variety to any cheese board and are extremely popular along the Garden Route.

Marianne's Millennium and Ricona are both mild cheeses with a semi-hard and open texture, which indicates that she used the traditional Dutch method for sweet-milk cheese. Neither of these cheeses is intended to be very strong or well-matured, which broadens their appeal for the average South African cheese lover. The Millennium is the most similar to a sweet-milk, and the Ricona is a soft spreading cheese. Both are natural and unflavoured, making them ideal table and ingredient cheeses, while the Caserio range, with its flavourful additives, is strictly a table cheese.

Marianne uses only hygienically produced raw milk, which lends a wonderfully full and earthy flavour to her cheese. Pasteurised milk cheese has become the norm in many parts of the world, but nothing beats the flavour of cheese made from raw milk, provided it only contains healthy bacteria.

Silver Lily Smoked Cheese

Silver Lily Ricona

Silver Lily Caserio

Simply Natural

Bedford, Eastern Cape
Nicky Prudhon

Lying along the banks of the Great Fish River, with the Winterberg range towering majestically in the distance, the farm Merinoville is home to cheesmaker Nicky Prudhon and her husband Christophe. When Nicky was a child growing up on a farm in Molteno, her mother began making Dutch-style cheese with surplus milk from their dairy, and it was there that Nicky first experienced cheesemaking. Today, Nicky makes cheese on the beautiful Eastern Cape farm that she, Christophe and their two-year-old son, Jacques, call home. Nicky continues what her mother taught her, but with the added knowledge that comes from being a qualified chef, and is producing cheese of an exceptionally high quality.

Nicky is passionate about food. After qualifying as a chef, she worked in restaurants in South Africa and in London. However, while on holiday in Thailand, she met and fell in love with French SCUBA instructor Christophe Prudhon. Nicky went on to complete her instructor's course and spent the next twelve years working with Christophe and travelling to exotic locations. Although she loved travelling, she always wanted to come back to South Africa to farm. 'I just had to convince a Frenchman to buy me a farm!' she jokes, but as Christophe happily drives past on a tractor waving at Jacques, it doesn't look like much persuading was necessary. Christophe also comes from a farming background in the Burgundy region of France.

Nicky and Christophe's 65-ha property – small by Eastern Cape standards – is located between Cradock and Cookhouse, along the Great Fish River, which means that it

Simply Natural Dutch Farmhouse

is irrigated. Both the farming business and Nicky's cheese business, Simply Natural, are run along simple, natural lines. The animals are kept on a natural diet, with no artificial products included, and the cheese is made in the most uncomplicated manner possible. The animals are fed no artificial products, growth stimulants or hormones, and no artificial additives, colouring or preservatives are added to the cheese.

The cows that they run are dual purpose, and the breeds are a mixture of beef cows – mainly Angus, but also some Friesland and Jersey. The bull is a Brown Swiss, fondly named 'Mr Brown', by Nicky. The calves stay with their mothers for up to eight months, unlike many dairy farms where calves are weaned young. Nicky believes that this process is important for a good-quality calf.

The cows are milked in the morning and cheesemaking begins immediately. Nicky is the sole cheesemaker on the farm, and uses a small building outside the main farmhouse as her cheesery. She meticulously writes down details and ideas on a blackboard, and times her processes to the second. On average, she makes about 10 kg of cheese per day, and sets one day aside for making feta. Fluent in Xhosa, and with the easygoing yet hardworking manner characteristic of farmers in the area, Nicky may come across as the typical Eastern Cape farm girl, but there is a great deal more to her than the stereotype allows. It is not easy to run a successful farm in the area, and Nicky and Christophe have worked extremely hard to get to where they are.

Ultimately, Nicky wants to develop her own cheese. At the moment, her produce is sold at several local local markets in the area, like Bedford, Port Elizabeth and Grahamstown, and her hard cheeses are sold in Cape Town and Johannesburg.

Kobus's Cheese Notes

When other girls were playing with dolls or checking the latest fashions, Nicky Broster was helping her mother make cheese on the family farm near the Stormberge. Today, as Nicky Prudhon, she is making cheese on Merinoville Farm outside Bedford. Here, husband Christophe farms citrus and produces the milk which Nicky transforms into her Dutch Farmhouse cheese. By using milk straight from the milking parlour, she saves on energy and prevents the possible growth of the dreaded psychotropic bacteria, which loves to multiply in fresh cold milk. Christophe's small herd grazes on natural pastures, which makes Nicky's cheeses stand out from other similar sweet-milk cheeses produced from milk sourced from more than one farm.

The Dutch Farmhouse is Nicky's best-known cheese, and is, as the name suggests, made in the Dutch style. This means that the curds are carefully washed with warm water once the initial separation has occurred, in order to lower the acidity and limit the acid development potential. It removes a certain portion of lactose from the curd moisture, which would normally have been converted to lactic acid. There is not an enormous difference in flavour to cheese made with unwashed curds, but Nicky has stayed with the cheesemaking tradition with which she grew up. She has begun to use microbial rennet, and although she admits that animal rennet is known to give a better flavour, she supports cheese as a vegetarian option. At the minimum, the cheese takes eight to ten weeks to mature, although it is preferably matured for up to six months.

Nicky's Dutch Farmhouse cheeses are made along the same traditional lines as those used by Dutch dairy farmers, and lucky cheese lovers in the Eastern Cape swear that hers taste better. Her natural cheese has the distinctive creamy and mild flavour so typical of washed curd cheeses. The texture is semi-hard, with just a few small eyes, which makes it an ideal snack and table cheese. The eyes are formed by gas produced by the natural bacteria in the milk, and lend a further subtle sweet flavour to the cheese.

Nicky sells a Dutch Farmhouse cheese in different varieties: plain, pecan nut, black pepper and chilli. It can be described as a version of Boerenkaas, which is a semi-hard cheese. In addition to the Dutch Farmhouse, Nicky also produces feta and ricotta, and is probably the only cheesemaker in South Africa making a semi-hard cheese with pecan nuts. The fresh nuts give a gastronomic appeal that the standard cumin or pepper additives don't. I remember the first time Nicky sent me samples of her cheese. We enjoyed it with Granny Smith apples, organic biltong from the Eastern Cape and Sauvignon Blanc made near the sea. It was a happy afternoon.

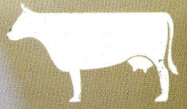

Simply Natural Feta

Swissland Cheese

Midlands, KwaZulu-Natal
Fran Isaac

Fran Isaac lives in what may be the most picturesque farm in the country, where she creates goat cheeses of exceptional quality. She grew up on a neighbouring farm, and continues with the dairy farming lifestyle in which she grew up. Although she lives high in the hills, surrounded by forests, Fran embodies a very straightforward and African lust for life. It is people like Fran that cement the common notion that the South African cheese revolution began in Natal. Having lived her whole life in KwaZulu-Natal, she has a deep pride and love for the area, and was a founder of the Midlands Meander, established by twelve people from the area in the 1980s.

It is not easy to reach Swissland Cheese, but Fran admits that she likes it that way. That is not to say she doesn't enjoy visitors, and many make the pilgrimage to her farm over the weekends. Fran's production and sales facility is built in the Swiss chalet vernacular, which adds to the charm of the property. Small chalets are perched on top of high green hills and snow-white Saanen goats roam freely. It really does seem like a small chunk of Switzerland.

Goats commonly suffer from wet feet in damp conditions, which can result in painful problems. Because Fran's farm is in the Midlands mist belt, it is often foggy and wet, but she overcame the problem by building simple yet ingenious structures that her goats can stand on without their feet getting wet. Her goat pens are also raised, so that their waste falls through the slatted floor, and is cycled onto the land as fertiliser.

Fran's approach to her land is a holistic one; her goats are hormone-free and roam the pastures grazing on lush grass, never confined to small pens. The same philosophy goes into her cheese, which is free of colourants and chemicals. Fran creates beautiful, delicious and award-winning goat's cheeses that are highly sought after. She is constantly experimenting, and has made her own smoker, in which she smokes her soft chèvre.

The cheesemaking facility at Swissland seems more like fun than hard work, and it isn't uncommon to overhear Fran and the women she employs enjoying a good laugh in the cheese room. Fran runs her farm professionally and looks after her animals with excellent husbandry. She also keeps the chalet in spotless condition, and her pastures are immaculately manicured. Her cheeses are perfectly moulded and each is as flawless as the next. As good as she is at the rougher aspects of farming, she's equally adept at the small details and aesthetics. Don't be misled by the rough-and-tumble aspect, because there is an astute precision. That is why she makes such good cheese.

Kobus's Cheese Notes

Every time I visit Fran Isaac at Swissland Cheese, I come across wild buck crossing the narrow and steep dirt road. Before I reach the cheesery at the top of the hill, the Saanen goats greet me with the typical inquisitive facial expression of a milk goat. The manicured lawns of the pleasant picnic area and the Swiss-style building create an area of tranquillity that is deceiving. I should not forget that keeping and milking 75 goats and making cheese are never-ending tasks.

Fran started farming milk goats and making cheese at the end of the 1990s, which makes her one of the goat's milk cheese pioneers in South Africa. Visitors to the Midlands Meander immediately liked her cheese, and when she exhibited at the very first National Cheese Festival outside Franschhoek, Cape cheese lovers also fell in love with her delicately flavoured soft cheeses. Most of her cheese is sold on the farm, and the rest is delivered to delicatessens and restaurants in KwaZulu-Natal and Cape Town.

Today, Swissland makes ten different goat's milk cheeses, but I still like the very first three the best, probably because I was so impressed when I first tasted them. The lactic-curd Sainte Maure-style cheese, which was my introduction to Fran's cheeses, has the typical acid-salt balance and walnut aroma to which I became accustomed in the Poitou-Charentes region of western France. I prefer to enjoy it when it is young and still has that lemony fresh and slightly nutty flavour. At this stage, it is equally good as a table cheese to savour on your tongue, or warm in a *chèvre chaud*, that ubiquitous French salad. With age, the somewhat grainy texture gets more crumbly and the flavour more aromatically herbaceous; the best way to eat it at this stage is to gently grill it on fresh ciabatta with a dollop of fynbos honey. The Swissland Camembert is, without a doubt, among the top goat Camemberts made in South Africa. Its damp leaf-and-mushroom flavour impresses every time, and its thin edible rind is evenly covered in a delicate layer of pure white mould. If left to ripen gracefully, it develops a smooth soft texture. Wine masters can put the best red wines in front of me, but I will enjoy a light Pinot Noir with a Swissland Camembert every time. On second thought, I have enjoyed it with a Cap Classique and it was just as good.

The Swissland Drakensberg is another lactic-curd cheese, made in a log shape and rolled in black ash, which contrasts beautifully with the white cheese. This little cheese is a must for any well-thought-out cheese platter, firstly because of its fresh, slightly acidic taste, and secondly because it is just so lovely to look at.

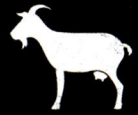

Swissland Drakensberg

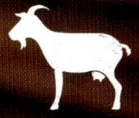

Swissland Tombrini

Zandam Cheese

Durbanville, Western Cape
Mauro delle Donne

In the 1960s a farm just outside Durbanville was the setting for a real Italian love story. A young Italian man, Matteo delle Donne, had arrived in South Africa looking for work. He had heard of this 'land of opportunity' at the bottom of Africa through his father and uncle, who had been captured in Abyssinia during the Second World War and had been brought to South Africa as prisoners of war. Matteo arrived in South Africa and began calling at a nearby poultry farm to buy empty feed bags, which he resold to the mills.

Another Italian man, an ex-prisoner of war, worked on the poultry farm. He had left a wife and daughter behind in Italy, and his wife was becoming frustrated. His daughter Iolanda, happily living in Italy, was courting an Italian man, who eventually broke her heart. Iolanda's mother asked her to fetch her father and bring him back to Italy, and Iolanda, happy to go on an adventure, agreed. Inevitably, while on the farm with her father, she met Matteo. Needless to say, Iolanda didn't leave South Africa. She returned to Italy thirteen years later with three children and a happy husband.

Today, Matteo and Iolanda's son, Mauro delle Donne, runs Zandam, the highly successful family cheese company. When Mauro was growing up on the farm, there was, in true Italian tradition, a small cheesery on the side. Iolanda would make mozzarella and other Italian cheeses, and young Mauro became familiar with cheesemaking.

In 1979 the poultry business was sold to a larger corporation, but the farm continued with pigs, dairy and cheese. Mauro and his brother Tino joined the business in 1988,

Zandam Mascarpone

and the brothers realised that they needed to expand the business in order to make provision for two families. They focused their energies on expanding cheese production.

Mauro has been running Zandam, together with a dedicated and enthusiastic staff, since Tino left the business in 2001, and the company has gone from strength to strength. Twenty thousand litres of milk is processed, and over two tonnes of mozzarella generated, each day. With a focus on Italian cheeses, the products are extremely popular in the South African food industry, and Zandam has won awards for its mascarpone and ricotta.

Mauro points out his original 200-litre vat, dwarfed by the 16 000-litre vats in the factory. He is still passionate about cheesemaking, and uses the smaller vat to develop new products and experiment with recipes when he has free time.

Much of the cheesemaking at Zandam today is mechanised. Mauro, however, will proudly tell visitors that their cheese is just as authentic as handmade Italian cheese. There are no preservatives or colourants: 'With cheese, there are no shortcuts,' Mauro explains. 'The machines just make it easier.' This becomes clear as he demonstrates the process of stretching mozzarella. This is a key stage, as it changes the flavour as well as the texture of the final product, but it requires an enormous amount of time and exertion. The exact same process occurs in the giant silver machine that churns out bricks of fresh mozzarella by the second.

Although Mauro loves cheese and cheesemaking, he realised that in order to make the business successful, he needed to think like a businessman. Despite the scale and the success of Zandam today, Mauro will not stray from his Italian roots, and can't resist showing off his private cold room, filled with Parma hams, salamis, cheeses and olives, all grown and produced on the Zandam farm. The small business of making cheese in the Delle Donne family has become a thriving and award-winning business today, because of the two young Italians who found each other and fell in love in a far-off country.

Kobus's Cheese Notes

Mauro delle Donne was born next to *il caseificio* (the dairy), grew up in it and lived next to it for more years than he cares to remember. Why am I not surprised that he understands cheesemaking and makes a range of classic Italian cheeses of outstanding quality? Although the humble Mauro will deny it, the reputations of many Italian restaurants in the greater Cape Town area were built on, and are still supported by, the quality mozzarella, pecorino, ricotta and mascarpone from Zandam Cheese. The deep and thorough understanding of cheesemaking which Mauro and his loyal staff possess is the reason why Zandam cheeses have been awarded many prizes and are appreciated by their loyal clients.

The moist and slightly grainy ricotta is freshly made from the whey of mozzarella, and is dispatched to clients as early as the following day to optimise the fresh milky flavour. The manufacturing method for ricotta sounds simple: the whey is cooked to 85°C, and almost immediately after, a small quantity of citric acid is added. The proteins separate from the whey and float to the surface, to be scooped off using a strainer. Easy? No. To make good fluffy ricotta with a smooth, fine texture, and a taste more sweet than acidic, is something that Mauro understands and does very well. For years, the taste buds of our dinner guests have been taught a gastronomic lesson by a pear and honey ricotta tart made with luscious ricotta from Zandam. The secret, according to my wife, is the ricotta.

In a world where many pasta dishes have to endure inferior grating cheese, Zandam's pecorino is ambrosial. Italy has probably around 30 different pecorino cheeses, mostly made from ewe's milk, although some can contain a mixture of ewe's and goat's milk. The Zandam pecorino is made from cow's milk, as in many New World countries where sheep's milk is not plentiful, and can therefore not be compared directly with that in Italy. The hard and compact texture makes it ideal to grate over a freshly made linguini or risotto, or to be enjoyed with with walnuts and fresh pears. At six to eight months matured, it grates easily and is not crumbly or crunchy as in the case of *stagionato* (aged for 9 to 12 months). Through the years, I have eaten Zandam pecorino in *fresco* and semi-*stagionato* styles when it has a softer texture and milder flavour, and I like them all. Zandam also makes a pepato, where the pecorino includes whole black peppercorns, as in the south of Italy.

Mauro's bocconcini, or little *fior de latte* balls, is a standard item in my cheese-loving house. A few of these soft balls with tomato, fresh basil, olive oil and black pepper is a meal for a king – and for me.

Zandam Pepato

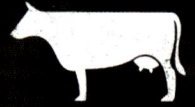

Zandam Ricotta

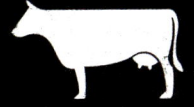

Zandam Bocconcini

Cheese Awards

The cheesemakers featured here have won various South African and international awards since 2006.

Belnori

Winner of 2012 South African Dairy Awards for Halloumi, Pepper Pot and Summertime Goat's Milk Feta; Coeur de Crème and St Catherine's Camembert; Tanglewood; Highvelder Classic; Kalembe; Savannah; Savannah Sec; Sonata; Feta Pecora; Serengeti; Halloumi Pecora

Winner of a 2012 World Cheese Silver Award for Plain Feta

Dalewood

Finalist of 2012 Eat In Produce Award for Languedoc

Winner of 2012 Sunday Times Top 20 Most Favourite Artisanal Cheeses in South Africa

Winner of 2006, 2007 and 2008 World Cheese Gold Award for Huguenot, as well as a 2010 Super Gold Award Medal

2011 Slow Food Artisanal Cheese Citation for Huguenot

2011 SA Dairy South African Champion Award for Huguenot

Foxenburg Estate

Winner of 2009 World Cheese Silver Award for Foxtail

Winner of 2009 South African Dairy Award for Shepherd

Winner of 2012 South African Dairy Award for Chabris

Ganzvlei Dairy

Winner of a 2011 Slow Food Award for Ganzvlei Vastrap

Winner of a 2012 South African Dairy Award for Ganzvlei Vastrap

Gay's Dairy

Winner of a 2009 Slow Food Award

Goat Peter

Winner of a 2012 South African Dairy Award for Valais, Grison and La Punt

Winner of a 2012 Qualité Award for Grison

Healey's Farmhouse Cheese

Winner of 2006, 2009 World Cheese Gold Awards and a 2011 World Cheeses Bronze Award

Hijke Cheeses

Winner of a 2012 South African Dairy Award for Parmesan

Indezi River Cheese Company

Winner of a 2012 South African Dairy Award for Indezi Pontsula and Dutch Gouda with Cumin

Klein River Cheese

Winner of a 2012 South African Dairy Awards for Havarti, Grana, Gruyère and Matured Gruyère

Winner of the 2012 South African Dairy Championships Award for Best Product of the Year for the Franschoek Angelot

Ovis Angelica

Slow Food citations for Labneh and Jan Groentjie

Swissland Cheese

Winner of a 2012 South African Dairy Award for Brie

Zandam

Winner of 2012 South African Dairy Awards for Mozzarella, Smoked Mozzarella, Pepato and Mascarpone and Ricotta

The Best Cheesemakers & Cheese Shops in South Africa

Eastern Cape

Simply Natural

PO Box 129,
Bedford
cnprudhon@gmail.com

Latteria eRhini

Elangeni Market,
Grahamstown
virginia.davide@gmail.com

Free State

Beaconsfield Cheesery

PO Box 72,
Hofmeyer 5930
clord@vodamail.co.za

Ovis Angelica

PO Box 151,
Smithfield 9966
eva@sasheepdairy.co.za

Bon Appetit

Post House Corner,
Main Street, Clarens
vkneppert@vodamail.co.za

Gauteng

Belnori

PO Box 7246,
Petit 1512
www.belnori.co.za

Goat Peter

PO Box 33,
Hekpoort 1790
www.goatpeter.com

Hijke Cheeses

PO Box 11434,
Erasmuskloof 0048
iti03547@mweb.co.za

Cheese Gourmet

Corner 7th Street and 3rd Avenue
Linden, Johannesburg
sacheese@gmail.com

KwaZulu-Natal

Chrissie's Country Cheese

PO Box 36,
Eston 3740

Indezi River Cheese Company

PO Box 84,
Balgowan 3275
info@indezi.co.za

Swissland Cheese

PO Box 80,
Balgowan 3275
franvermaak@mweb.co.za

Mpumalanga

Cavalier Cheese

30 Waterfall Avenue,
Riverside Industrial Park
Mbombela (Nelspruit)
info@cavcheese.co.za

North West

For a course in cheesemaking:

Grootplaas De Rust Cheese Academy
near Hartbeespoort, North West
www.cheeseacademy.co.za
info@cheeseacademy.co.za

Western Cape

Aidan Pomario

PO Box 71,
Hoekwil 6538
aidanpomario@gmail.com

Alpine Goats Cheese

PO Box 136,
Napier 7270
info@goats-cheese.co.za

Buffalo Ridge

PO Box 941,
Wellington 7654
buffaloridge@iafrica.com

Cloud Cottage

PO Box 38,
Avontuur 6490

Dalewood

PO Box 95,
Simondium 7670
www.dalewood.co.za

Foxenburg Estate

PO Box 672,
Wellington 7654
marianne@foxenburg.co.za

Ganzvlei Dairy

PO Box 251,
Knysna 6570
ganzvlei@icon.co.za

Gay's Dairy

PO Box 137,
Prince Albert 6930

Healey's Farmhouse Cheese

PO Box 2093,
Somerset West 7129
www.healeys.co.za

Klein River Cheese

PO Box 13,
Stanford 7210
kleinriver@telkomsa.net

Silver Lily Cheese Farm

PO Box 1847,
George 6530
silverlily@lantic.net

Zandam Cheese

PO Box 94,
Durbanville 7551
willie@zandamcheese.co.za

Cheese Head

Timberlake Farm Stall,
N2 between Wilderness and Sedgefield
cheesehead@vodamail.co.za

The Real Cheese Shop

Bishop Corner, 217 Lower Main Road
Observatory, Cape Town
getstuffed@mweb.co.za

Saucisse

The Old Biscuit Mill
Woodstock, Cape Town

Constantia Cheesery

Corner Frederick Selous Avenue
and Collette Close,
Constantia, Cape Town
janselan@absamail.co.za

Index